MINDFUL WILLPOWER

MINDFUL WILLPOWER

POWERFUL MINDFULNESS
PRACTICES TO INCREASE
SELF-CONTROL, GET FOCUSED,
AND BUILD GOOD HABITS

SAMARA SEROTKIN, PSYD

ROCKRIDGE
PRESS

For general information on our other products and services or to obtain technical support, please contact our Customer Care Department within the United States at (866) 744-2665, or outside the United States at (510) 253-0500.

Rockridge Press publishes its books in a variety of electronic and print formats. Some content that appears in print may not be available in electronic books, and vice versa.

Interior and Cover Designer: Eric Pratt
Art Producer: Hannah Dickerson
Editors: Seth Schwartz and Mo Mozuch
Production Editor: Emily Sheehan

Illustrations used under license from Shutterstock.com

ISBN: Print 978-1-64876-026-6 | eBook 978-1-64876-027-3
R0

In this expansive and unknowable universe, I ground myself in my local constellation and Northern Stars. To David, Henry, and Meadow—Thank you for supporting my tiny light in the sky. May this book contribute in some small way to a better world in which everyone has more opportunity to thrive.

CONTENTS

Introduction

Since you picked up this book, I imagine you are interested in becoming more effective at making changes in your life. Perhaps you're hoping to lose some weight, exercise more, or just generally treat your body with more respect. Maybe you want to change your behavior around technology use. Or perhaps you want to develop a mindfulness meditation practice. If so, then you've probably learned from firsthand experience just how hard it can be to make sustainable changes in your life.

Regardless of your aims, making real change can be challenging, especially when you factor in your daily habits, which serve to support your behaviors. Habits, by definition, happen when we're not paying attention. It's hard to notice them unless we *practice* paying attention in the present moment. The background mental scripts we all have running in our heads create a sort of framework or scaffolding onto which we hang our everyday routines and habits. If you've ever found yourself thinking the same repetitive thoughts when you're commuting, washing dishes, or showering, or are waking up in the middle of the night, running over situations in your head on repeat, you know what I mean. Thought habits can be *strong*. And they have an enormous impact on our perception and interpretation of everyday life. We all have our blind spots, and they tend to crop up in some of these thought habits. As long as we remain stuck in them, our habits generally don't budge either.

Here's an example from my own life. Recently I'd fallen into a pattern of leaving dirty dishes in the sink overnight. It was an easy habit to develop, especially considering that my family has been spending a lot more time together at home, and consequently, we've been using a lot more dishes. (I'm writing this book during the COVID-19 pandemic of 2020.) Washing the dishes had gotten a tad overwhelming. Plus, even though the dishes were usually my responsibility, I fell into a habit of leaving them for the morning so I could squeeze in some more quality time with my husband and kids in the evening. The problem was that in the morning my kitchen was a depressing sight. I really like having a clean kitchen to start my day, but I was waking up to sticky, stinky messes and a nagging sense of "I should make a different choice tonight."

But then, when the evening rolled around, I was quick to buy into the narrative I spun in my head about why I deserved to leave the dishes in the sink and wait until tomorrow. In the morning, facing another mess, I was left wondering where my willpower went. When habits don't budge, it's handy to blame willpower. When you see others struggle to make changes in their lives, do you ever think to yourself, "They just don't have enough willpower to make it happen?"

How about you? Have you ever used a lack of willpower as a way to explain a past failure? "I just didn't have enough willpower to turn down that extra cookie." Or "I really was going to go to the gym, but then I walked past my favorite restaurant and just didn't have enough willpower to stop myself." As a human being, surely you can relate to this.

Mindfulness meditation is a game-changer when it comes to making personal changes. It's an ancient practice with modern practical and even urgent implications. Mindfulness is the practice of carpe diem. It is literally the practice of seizing the moment to approach it with all you've got. Mindfulness is about increasing your ability to clearly access the present moment without judgment or assumptions. And it is only from this place that you can enact real changes in your life. When you sit in silence, and finally are able to access the space between thoughts and let your mind rest for a moment . . . what will you do with that?

"What is most personal is most universal." I first heard these words many years ago, and it has repeatedly proven itself to be true throughout my work. The quotation comes from

Carl Rogers, a humanistic psychologist whom I continue to be inspired by today.

I'm a clinical psychologist and life coach, and I've been in the business of helping people convert inspiration into action for more than 20 years. My approach to my life and my work is firmly grounded in my own mindfulness meditation practice, which has been with me in various forms since I first encountered it in my early 20s.

In my job, clients come to me seeking change. Inevitably, whether they want help with navigating depression or anxiety or they are looking to change their trajectory in life by losing weight or achieving new goals, their thought habits tend to play a major supporting role in keeping them stuck where they are and blocking them from making progress. However, as we work together, they often find that their habits can also be their friends, and this paves the way to make change flow more easily. Mindfulness meditation is the tool that helps make those kinds of changes more accessible.

All change happens in the present moment.

Practicing mindfulness can help you intentionally build a structure to support the kind of changes you want to make in your life. In many ways, that's what self-control is really about. In the context of this book, it's about developing the ability to recognize thought habits that you've outgrown or that you're better off without and to actually practice disengaging from antiquated thought habits in real time until you've developed new habits—ones that you've developed intentionally—in their places. Wherever you want to apply willpower and self-control, mindfulness will serve you well.

This book will guide you in developing a mindfulness meditation practice and to use those skills to increase your ability to access the present moment with open, nonjudgmental awareness. Then, you can plant new habits that you wish to cultivate with intentionality. The greatest willpower is accessed from grounded self-awareness in the present moment so you can move forward with wise action.

You will find invitations to practice throughout this book. I encourage you to actually carve out the time to try these practices. In many ways your ability to act with self-control in the present moment is limited only by your ability to truly access the present moment. This means that showing up for your mindfulness practice at the most basic level is an essential foundation for you to make sustainable changes.

Mindfulness meditation is the practice of opening the door to the present moment. It's hard to do—downright impossible—without some solid practice. However, thanks to the phenomenon of neuroplasticity (which I'll cover in more detail later in this book), our brains have the ability to rewire themselves. Mindfulness practice is just like building a muscle: The more you exercise it, the stronger and more robust it becomes.

Also, it's important to note that mindfulness meditation is never about perfection. It's only about *progress*. All you need to do is show up for the practice and try. The practice will meet you where you are, ready to welcome you with nonjudgmental awareness. There are no quality markers other than showing up and practicing. As you'll see, when you break through whatever is blocking you from your mindfulness practice, you'll also unlock doors in other areas of your life.

This book was written with the intention of making the practice accessible to you and applicable to your daily life and what's most important to you. Wherever you want more willpower and however you want to apply more self-control, this book is here to help you get there, one step at a time.

CHAPTER 1

THE MINDFUL WAY

One of my favorite mindfulness meditation teachers is Thich Nhât Hanh, who was nominated for the Nobel Peace Prize by Martin Luther King Jr. in 1967. He sometimes likes to describe the importance and urgency of developing a mindfulness meditation practice by using the metaphor of *cultivating a garden.* If you've ever tried gardening, you know what happens if you water and fertilize every single plant that tries to sprout in your garden bed: You end up with a tangled mess of weeds and a lack of resources for the plants you truly wish to cultivate. Those weeds suck up all the valuable resources. They rob the water and nutrients from the soil as well as the limited and therefore valuable sun space in the plot. There's no room or resources for the plants you actually want to cultivate. The same is true for our minds: You've got to be careful about what kind of thoughts you choose to engage with and allow to take up space.

We all get stuck in thought habits, those narratives that run on repeat in the backs of our minds when we're doing other things, like washing the dishes, commuting, or showering. These thought habits have a tremendous impact on our moods and attitudes and can influence the way we perceive the world by creating cognitive biases. These thought habits are the framework we structure our lives and personalities around. They become our assumptions. And assumptions, when left unchecked, can create cognitive biases that can become downright dangerous.

In this chapter, you'll begin to learn why and how to cultivate your garden. We'll look at the link between mindfulness meditation, willpower, and self-control. We'll explore in detail the practice of mindfulness meditation, and you'll learn techniques to help you squeeze a mindfulness meditation practice into your potentially busy life. I'll describe common barriers my clients have encountered in developing their own practices and give you access to the tools they have found most helpful in creating their own practices.

We'll start by looking at why you would want to develop a mindfulness meditation practice, by exploring the research about the power and the benefits of mindfulness meditation.

MINDFUL WILLPOWER

Willpower and self-control are just terms to describe one's ability to control oneself not just in isolation but also when encountering everyday challenges and real-world problems.

Mindfulness meditation functions as a potent tool to increase your ability to apply willpower and self-control in the present moment. Whether you're trying to improve your relationship with food, develop a more consistent exercise routine, or change how you feel when you look in the mirror, these habits all involve wanting more willpower and self-control. Mindfulness meditation is the tool to supercharge your efforts to get there.

Why is self-control so challenging? There are many things that get in our way. We all encounter things like lack of focus. Focus seems harder and harder to cultivate in today's turbo-speed world. With so many devices grabbing for snippets of our attention, our brains are out of practice at maintaining sustained attention for extended periods of time. Bad habits are really hard to break. They happen, by definition, when we're not paying attention to them. They're what our brains do on autopilot while we're doing other things. So getting started with changing anything can be challenging because of the inherent power of old habits.

One of the most troublesome of old habits is procrastination. Procrastination essentially lets us kick the problem down the road until a later time. Once you get into a habit of procrastination, it's easy to lose track of long-term benefits over short-term gains. *Habits gain momentum.* Procrastination gains force particularly quickly, especially in the face of so many opportunities for instant gratification.

Your emotions affect your ability to use self-control and willpower, and it can be easy to let emotions get the best of you. When emotions get big, your fight-or-flight system gets activated. (This is your body's primal panic response.) Your prefrontal cortex is the center of impulse control and your ability to choose long-term benefits over short-term gains. When fight-or-flight is activated, the prefrontal cortex shuts down as the brain reallocates resources to rally support for the call to action being heralded by the amygdala, the home of the fight-or-flight system. The shutting down of the prefrontal cortex allows our emotions to explode out of control and makes self-control and willpower feel completely elusive. Once emotions get huge, they can be hard to regulate, and the lure of the promised relief of instant gratification becomes amplified.

Fortunately, your prefrontal cortex is also the same part of the brain that grows in gray matter density and power when you practice mindfulness meditation regularly. I'll talk more about that later in the book.

THE POWER OF MINDFULNESS

There are many forms of meditation, but mindfulness meditation is the one we'll focus on in this book. Mindfulness meditation is the practice of cultivating an attitude of mindfulness. This means you try to bring *nonjudgmental awareness* to the present moment, something that is often easier said than done. It involves cultivating the ability to be aware of when you start engaging in thoughts as well as developing the practice of resisting the urge to become absorbed in them. If that sounds simple, it's because it is. But, *don't mistake simple for easy.* Mindfulness meditation is anything but easy. Just try quietly sitting in the space between thoughts for a few minutes by paying attention to a single whole breath without getting lost in thought. It's harder than it sounds. But the good news is that with practice, even just a few minutes a day, you can cultivate a mindfulness practice. In addition, mindfully engaging in creative projects can be an enjoyable and relaxing way to connect to the practice.

When we practice mindfulness meditation, we're trying to experience one moment at a time with our full attention. We resist the urge to get swept away by thoughts, and work to apply our full attention to as many moments as we can. The thing is, though, our brains love to find things to think about. When we try to focus on one breath at a time, our brains quickly want to skip ahead, assuming we know what each breath will feel like, so they can move on to thinking about other things. It's tricky to work against this conditioning and really stay with one moment at a time, but with practice, it becomes continually easier and the benefits are worth it.

As a therapist, I try to mindfully listen to my clients. This means offering them my full attention as much as possible. When my mind wanders to opinions, hypotheses, or what I am seeing outside the window, I notice the moment of distraction and gently bring my attention back to listening to my clients with as much nonjudgmental awareness as I can muster. It's natural for me to have thoughts and opinions, but to do my job well I need to avoid getting distracted by them when I am with my clients.

Although there has been a surge in interest in mindfulness meditation over the past decade, the practice has been around far longer than that. Mindfulness dates back to 1500 BCE in Hinduism under the context of yoga. Variations of it have been practiced in almost all major religions, although it's well-known that the Buddha adopted the practice, and mindfulness meditation has become a cornerstone of Buddhism.

I am no Buddhist scholar, but my basic understanding of one aspect of Buddhism is that Buddhists believe that human nature leads us to want to get attached to things staying a certain way. We like our habits. We get attached to the status quo. We generally don't like to lose the things we like, and we almost always want to get rid of the things that cause us pain. However, this attachment is problematic because we can't change the past, and we have little idea what the future will hold. Yet, we get attached to things being or staying a certain way—and then they change. Change always happens; in fact, the one thing we can count on in this world is impermanence. Nothing lasts forever. Yet, once we are able to accept impermanence, we become able to live in the present moment more fully and completely than we ever have before.

Buddhism is a religion based on the Buddha's teachings; however, you can adapt the basic practice of mindfulness without taking on the religious aspects. Dr. Jon Kabat-Zinn is an author, clinician, researcher, and the founder of mindfulness-based stress reduction (MBSR). MBSR is a program that has brought secular mindfulness into the lives of many people and organizations. Kabat-Zinn took a scientific approach to the traditional practice, prompting research on and subsequent evidence of the role mindfulness plays in emotional regulation. With a background in molecular biology, Kabat-Zinn designed an MBSR program for patients he worked with in a hospital. He began collecting data early on to test the effectiveness of the program, which quickly grew in popularity. Kabat-Zinn is widely credited with the rise of mindfulness as a secular practice, and his program has now been taught to more than 20,000 people.

Secular mindfulness is really about developing *attention resilience*—exercising the ability to be present without getting swept away by unconscious thought habits. It's about holding your open attention in the present moment without judgment. Some religions, like Buddhism, have guidelines about what kind of attention to cultivate and what is best to do with that attention. But as a secular mindfulness practitioner, it's up to you to choose. As you learn to become more present, you can choose what to do with your attention as you develop awareness of your thought habits and become more intentional with your focus.

Research-Backed Benefits

Mindfulness meditation practice, once only used by monks and deep meditators, has become increasingly accessible to all kinds of people all over the world throughout recent decades. Much of its publicity in the West came from the research pioneered by Kabat-Zinn whose MBSR program has been the subject of much research and has been taught in corporate settings, the military, hospitals, prisons, and retreats. It's even inspired the development of other programs, like Mindfulness-Based Relapse Prevention and Mindfulness-Based Eating Awareness Training.

In recent years, the number of research studies on mindfulness has soared. Mindfulness is frequently covered in the mainstream media, and there are smartphone apps and online resources to help you practice it. Celebrities and CEOs are practicing mindfulness, and a growing number of companies are offering mindfulness classes to their employees. Schools are integrating mindfulness training into their curriculum as early as kindergarten. When you look closely at the evidence, it's easy to see why. The long list of benefits connected with mindfulness includes reduced stress; improved sleep; increased emotional well-being; enhanced memory, focus, and creativity; and greater self-compassion, subjective well-being, and overall satisfaction with life. Other positive effects include reductions in anxiety, depression, emotional reactivity, perceived stress, and burnout.

One of the many exciting things that happen when you practice mindfulness meditation is that you engage your brain's *neuroplasticity*. Neuroplasticity is your brain's ability to reorganize itself by forming new neural pathways and connections. In other words, practicing mindfulness meditation on a regular basis has a measurable and direct impact on the structure of your brain. Certain predictable changes occur and can be viewed in as few as eight weeks.

First of all, your prefrontal cortex grows in gray matter density. Gray matter is the basic stuff that makes up your brain. When the density increases, that means there are more brain cells concentrated there. Your prefrontal cortex is where your thinking brain resides. It's also where impulse control, abstract thought, and long-term planning happen, so you are literally bulking up in this area. Plus, the connections between this part of the brain and the rest of the brain increase in number.

At the same time, the part of your brain associated with fight-or-flight decreases in gray matter density. And the connections between it and the rest of the brain decrease in number. In other words, the fight-or-flight part of your brain gets out of the driver's seat and your prefrontal cortex gets in. Plus, there is a small section of your brain associated with meta-cognition or meta-awareness, which is the awareness of thoughts themselves. This part of the brain also grows in gray matter density. Awareness is a skill you are practicing and getting better at.

This process of cultivating awareness and developing *attention resilience* can also be likened to a form of mental fitness training. Much like when you engage in a repetitive action to build muscle at the gym, the practice of mindfulness meditation done regularly strengthens the parts of your brain that are connected to things like time and task management, abstract thought, and even emotional intelligence.

As a psychologist, I use mindfulness meditation in my therapy practice to help people get in touch with the habitual thought patterns that contribute to their suffering or inability to thrive. Over the years, I've seen many lives transformed by people changing their relationship with their thoughts. The more you practice mindfulness, the better you get at noticing habitual thoughts *as they are happening*, not just in retrospect. With this awareness, you can make more conscious choices about which thoughts to engage with and which ones to leave behind, increasing your willpower and self-control.

Everyday Practice

The key to accessing these benefits is developing a consistent practice. Although a formal mindfulness practice is usually done with focused attention on the breath, it doesn't need to begin or end there. There is a host of informal mindfulness practices you can use in addition to a formal practice to fit some real-life practice into your day. Informal practices do not replace a formal practice, but they can really help you get the most out of mindfulness.

You can practice being mindful when you're in line at a store, going for a walk, or folding laundry, or while you're engaging in a creative process like coloring, woodworking, or cooking. By pausing your normal mental triaging process as you take in information, you can engage directly with what is happening in the present moment. And by cultivating a beginner's mind and becoming curious about what you will experience from moment to moment, you can be present in where you are at any given moment. Like a child, you can view the present moment through fresh eyes, momentarily allowing yourself to see beyond what you think you know about a situation. You can literally engage with the world around you with more openness and creativity.

Tasks like washing dishes, trimming a hedge, or commuting can be an opportunity either to ruminate or to clear the mind. As your hands are busy doing something you don't need to pay attention to, your mind can either jump into its usual background scripts, or it can let go for a few minutes and practice being present. Creative practices in particular help me clear the clutter in my head and engage with the present more directly. I call these creative and daily practices my "windshield wiper" practices. They help me "clean my lens" so that I can see more clearly and, hopefully, see beyond my biases and habitual ways of thinking. We'll explore these practices in more detail later in this book.

Again, mindfulness isn't about being perfect. It isn't about trying to stop having thoughts or even about changing your thoughts. Rather, it's simply about recognizing when you're distracted and then coming back to the present moment, and then practicing coming back to the present moment again and again. *There's no need to judge yourself for being pulled away or getting distracted.* Thinking is an essential part of being human. Our awesome brains love to think and reflect on things. A mindfulness practice is about getting better at noticing your thoughts when you are having them and making more conscious choices about what to do in response to them.

Essentially, mindfulness is about responding instead of reacting. With regular practice, mindfulness can actually rewire the brain and make it easier to focus your thoughts where you choose to, rather than where they automatically and unconsciously take you. And in many ways, it gets easier the more you do it. Mindfulness meditation engages neuroplasticity so your brain rewires itself to support the practice and you can take your inner experience from chaotic to calm.

With even 10 minutes of mindfulness practice a day, you can effectively rewire your brain and take mindfulness from a state of practicing to a way of being. These are some tips that can help:

- ► Cultivate a particular attitude toward your experience. Foster an attitude that is curious, kind, and compassionate rather than evaluative or critical.

- ► Be intentional. Instead of letting your attention wander on autopilot, choose to be proactive with it.

- ► Pay attention to what is occurring in the present moment, including thoughts, feelings, and sensations. Notice when you are lost in thoughts about the past or future and return to the present.

TAMING THE MONKEY

It's tempting and normal to be taken for a ride on your train of thoughts while doing other things, such as writing an email to your boss or playing with your kids. But indulging in those random, looping thoughts takes you away from the present moment. It scatters your focus and keeps you from concentrating on and enjoying what is right in front of you. The more we engage with our looping thoughts—and most of us have been doing this most of our lives—the more conditioned the habit of unconsciousness becomes. Our brains have literally become hardwired to do other things—like ruminate on the past or worry about the future—while we're engaged in a task that would be better undertaken with our full attention. Meditation teachers often refer to this tendency as "monkey mind." Our minds are like monkeys jumping from tree to tree with no distinguishable focus or plan.

To get a better sense of what I mean by "monkey mind," try listening to silence for a few minutes. Try to let yourself simply observe the silence without thinking too much about it. If you're anything like me, your brain can seem almost repelled by the idea and will fill the space between thoughts with whatever idea seems shiniest at the moment. You could be contemplating a phone call you had earlier that day or figuring out a plot from a TV show you watched six months ago. Your attention may sail along your stream of consciousness with no real anchor or direction, sometimes looping into whirlpools that can keep you spinning for long periods of time.

Mindfulness meditation provides a light you can use to guide yourself through the storm and that, with practice, can become part of your brain's default patterns. Mindfulness can help you stay grounded and present. You can become aware of when you're getting pulled into a train of thoughts. You can learn how to make a conscious choice about what to do with your thoughts. And if you catch a train of thought you didn't intend to board, you know how to get off at the next station.

MINDFULNESS CLOCK

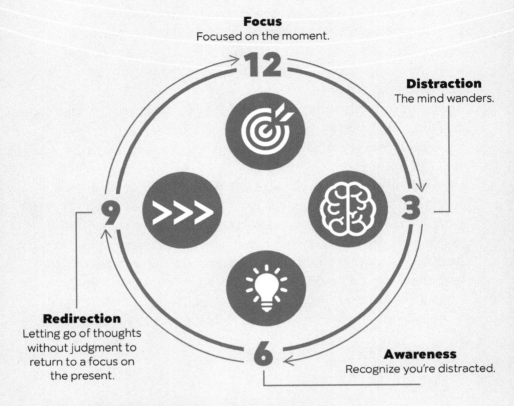

Focus
Focused on the moment.

Distraction
The mind wanders.

Awareness
Recognize you're distracted.

Redirection
Letting go of thoughts without judgment to return to a focus on the present.

How The Mindfulness Clock Works:

Focus: Bring your attention to what you're sensing and experiencing in the present moment. Start with a focus on your breath. Feel your body as it moves while you inhale and exhale, slowly and deeply.

Distraction: Inevitably, your mind will wander. You will likely get distracted before you're even aware you're distracted. This is a normal part of the process.

Awareness: You'll soon notice what the thoughts are that are distracting you from staying in the present moment.

Redirection: This is the most crucial step. Once you recognize your distracting thoughts, acknowledge them as such. Then, without judgment, let them go and free them from your mind so you can return to a focus on the moment.

Goal: The purpose of this exercise isn't to be better at breathing. It's to train your mind to regain control when your thoughts wander and you get off track. You may go through several cycles in a minute at first, that's OK. With practice you will soon get better at recognizing and redirecting your distracting thoughts.

On the surface, mindfulness meditation is really just about tracking your experience of the present moment through your senses. Your thoughts pull you away from the present moment. Those thoughts are usually about the past or the future, or they're analyzing something happening in the present moment. Either way, when you're meditating, your job is to focus on the present moment, notice when you get lost in thought, and gently redirect your attention to the present moment without judging yourself or the content of the thoughts.

Below the surface, there's a bit more to the process, and I like to describe it by using a model of a clock. I've used it on my website for years. There's a version of this exercise along with guided meditation recordings available there as well. This process is part of the mindfulness practices you'll find throughout the book.

You begin at 12 o'clock, focused on your experience of the present moment.

Soon, your mind gets lost in thought. This is 3 o'clock. You hang out at 3 o'clock for a little while before you are even aware that you're thinking.

Next comes 6 o'clock, that moment of awareness. This is when people often say things to themselves like "I'm thinking! I shouldn't be thinking! I'm no good at this," or "Maybe I'm just not cut out to meditate," or "Maybe I should try a different time of day or location." These thoughts have the potential of pulling you even further away from the present moment. Your job is to keep on moving around the circle to get to 9 o'clock. This is when you nonjudgmentally step aside from that thought as you redirect your attention to the present moment.

This 9 o'clock step can be trickier than it sounds. How do you "step aside from a thought"? It can be helpful to imagine placing your thought in a bubble and then just labeling it "thought." The content of the thought isn't important right now. Just label it "thought," no matter what you were thinking about, and let it go. As it floats away, know that if it's important it will come back to you eventually when you're not meditating. But now is the time to meditate and not engage in that thought.

You bring yourself back to 12 o'clock by reengaging with your senses. Maybe you take a deeper breath so you can feel it in your lungs and hear it in your ears. Either way you reengage your attention back on the present moment until 3 o'clock comes once again. Around and around you go.

The intent is to go around that circle as many times as you need to, not to stay at 12 o'clock as long as you can. Every time you make a circuit represents a thought from which you successfully disengaged. Think of it as training yourself to stay focused. It doesn't matter how many thoughts you have or how many times you go around the circle. What matters is that you notice you're distracted, and you bring your attention back to the present moment without judging yourself or the thoughts you are having. Rinse and repeat as many times as you need to during the time you set aside to meditate. That's it!

This clock analogy describes a formal mindfulness practice, which you practice on a regular basis. Think of it as your regular trip to the gym, morning run, or daily multivitamin. You don't need anything fancier than just this. That being said, I have packed the rest of this book with informal mindfulness practices where you can take your practice "off the cushion" and into everyday life. *Note:* While all of the activities in this book can be practiced in silence, many people prefer listening to guided recordings. Recordings of each exercise are available at SamaraSerotkin.com.

KEY TAKEAWAYS

► Mindfulness meditation is a powerful tool that can help you maintain the changes you make in your life.

► Research has proven that mindfulness meditation is associated with many benefits, ranging from reducing stress and improving sleep to boosting immune function and engaging neuroplasticity.

► Mindfulness meditation can be practiced almost anytime and anywhere, by just about everyone. And it doesn't cost a dime.

CHAPTER 2

UNDERSTANDING WILLPOWER

In this chapter, I'll introduce the concepts of willpower and self-control and what the current research says about them. We'll review some of what's known about willpower and explore some ways to apply this knowledge to your daily life. As you'll see, willpower is a simple word used to describe a complicated collection of impulses, responses, and actions that either lead us toward positive change or get in the way of it. We'll also look at what the research tells us about how to conserve and build up your willpower, so you have it when you need it the most.

WILLPOWER AND SELF-CONTROL

In the story "Cookies" from the classic children's book *Frog and Toad Together* by Arnold Lobel, we encounter Frog and Toad, two old friends, struggling with a familiar problem: They have a plate of cookies in front of them that they can't seem to stop eating. They both say that they need willpower, and their way of getting it involves making the cookies hard to access. Frog puts them in a box. But Toad points out that they could just open the box. So Frog tries tying the box shut, but Toad notes they could just cut the string. Finally, they both decide to give the cookies to the birds, which leaves them with their willpower, but no cookies. Toad ends the story by grumpily telling Frog that he can keep his willpower, and then goes home to bake a cake.

The Frog and Toad books have long been favorites in my household. I've read them to my two children so many times I've lost count. There was even a phase when my children repeatedly wanted me to come up with other examples of willpower. The chant "more willpower examples!" was an almost constant demand in our house for at least a year.

Although I truly enjoy all the Frog and Toad stories, I must admit that this one always left me feeling a bit frustrated. I wasn't satisfied with the message it gave my children about willpower and self-control. In fact, willpower is a really complex idea that has many components.

Willpower is often defined as the ability to control one's actions, or a strong determination to do something difficult. It sounds so simple, but what I know, based on my own experiences as well as those of my clients, is that the very concept of willpower can be problematic to so many. As a psychologist and coach, I help people catalyze change in their lives. So many of my clients blame their own lack of willpower for the suffering that they endure. It can feel disempowering, shaming, and even stigmatizing to be told that you just need more willpower to make a change, even if you're the one telling it to yourself. It implies the responsibility is entirely on you, and your failure to change simply represents a lack of willpower on your part.

Many people also seem to assume that willpower is a set trait, that either you have it or you don't, and that there is little you can do to change it. This is a toxic myth that this book will help debunk. Neuroscience has shown us that the brain is remarkably adaptable, and we can get better (or worse) at things we used to assume were fixed traits, including willpower.

The problems we encounter in today's world are complex. Sometimes, it seems like there is an infinite number of factors to weigh when making a decision, and *analysis paralysis* has become a real problem. There are so many moments throughout our daily lives that require us to force ourselves to get things done when we have to do them. All these tasks require the use of willpower.

Where does our willpower go? The demands of the day start from the moment you open your eyes in the morning, needing to resist the urge to stay in your cozy bed, and continue throughout the day as you make a dizzying number of decisions both big and small about where to focus your attention and spend your day. Research tells us that willpower is connected with academic success and achievement, higher self-esteem, better self-care habits, increased marital satisfaction, more effective leadership skills, and even greater financial security. How can we increase it?

In the next section, we'll take a closer look at what science says about willpower. We'll investigate more closely the relationship between our brains and our experience of willpower (or lack thereof). We'll also review some of the most current willpower research and the frameworks some of the current experts in the field use to explain and harness willpower—one of our most valuable resources. Like all resources, willpower is both depletable and replenishable. Let's start where it all begins: in the brain.

WILLPOWER AND THE BRAIN

We all have impulses and urges; we are all human, after all. But being human also means being part of humanity. And humans are, at our very core, tribal animals. We don't need to think too creatively to imagine situations in more primitive times where willpower became a desirable evolutionary trait. If the tribe is hungry, and you are a part of that tribe, it stands to reason that you are hungry as well. Now, imagine the tribe finally finds some food, but there isn't enough to go around. The tribe will reject you if you try to take more than your fair share. You have to control the survival instinct to eat in order to remain a part of the tribe with all the security associated with it.

In order to remain a part of the tribe, it's necessary to resist the urge to take all the food, even if you're strong enough (or the others are weak enough) for you to be able to overpower them and take it all for yourself.

The story gets even more interesting when we fold in what we know about evolution and natural selection. Survival of the fittest seems to be the name of the game when it comes to making it in this world. As humanity evolves, the genetic traits that help us survive evolve as well. This, when combined with neuroplasticity, reveals that humans have evolved to have very different brains than most other animal species.

One distinguishing factor of human brains is the enormous size of our prefrontal cortex. This part of the brain seems to have enjoyed exponential growth, growing at a rate much faster than the other parts of the brain. Over the past five million years, the size of the brain as a whole has tripled, but the prefrontal cortex itself has increased its size sixfold.

The prefrontal cortex is the part of the brain directly behind the forehead. When you look at a picture of the human brain from the side, it almost looks like it's become so dense it's folded in upon itself. This is also the last part of the brain to stop developing as we get older. The prefrontal cortex isn't fully formed until a person reaches about 25 years of age. Clearly the prefrontal cortex has been prioritized by our evolutionary tendencies. But why? The prefrontal cortex is the home of many functions essential for human life, from abstract thought to language to our sense of self. This section of the brain is also where willpower lives.

With all things neurology, it's important to remember that things are never as simple as they may seem. Neuroscience is a relatively new field, and the more we learn about it, the more mysteries and questions we uncover. We run the risk of oversimplifying things when we talk about specific sections of the brain being responsible for certain behaviors or actions, which are actually inherently quite complex. Let's look a little more at what we do and do not know about willpower and our brains.

If your prefrontal cortex is your evolved human brain, then your amygdala and the parts of the brain close to the brain stem are your primal brain. When your *fight-or-flight response*—the body's automatic reaction when it senses danger—is activated, your brain tends to reallocate resources away from the prefrontal cortex and down to the primal brain, which is where the fight-or-flight response lives. This way your brain has direct communication with your nervous system and can, for example, send urgent messages to your muscles to pull back your hand if it touches a hot surface. In these moments your brain doesn't have energy to spare for the parts of yourself that want to pause and contemplate the meaning of life. Your brain wants to take every shortcut it can to help you survive what it senses to be a dangerous situation.

Research has shown that brain patterns actually differ between people with high and low self-control. People with more self-control tend to have more activity in the prefrontal cortex. Another interesting difference is found in the part of the brain associated with processing desires and rewards: the ventral striatum. This area is more active in people who have lower amounts of self-control. Another way to look at this part of the brain is that the ventral striatum turns up the intensity of the sense of reward that comes with short-term gains, thus drowning out your long-term goals.

Stress also has an impact on many parts of your brain. For example, stress puts your brain in a reward-seeking state. This makes you crave things that you think will make you feel better. Unfortunately, what you think will make you feel better often isn't what will actually make you feel better. Therefore, stress can be the cause of many bad habits.

Some research suggests willpower is associated with lower glucose levels in the brain. Lower glucose levels lead the body to divert resources to stabilize blood sugar levels, which can leave us feeling hungry, irritable, and downright *hangry*. Part of the willpower puzzle is providing a consistent source of healthy fuel for the body and brain, which means avoiding blood sugar spikes and crashes. One important way to accomplish this is to eat a healthy and balanced diet and avoid highly processed simple carbohydrates and extreme hunger.

WILLPOWER RESEARCH

It would be remiss of me to talk about the research behind willpower without starting with the famous *marshmallow test*. You may have heard about these experiments in which preschoolers were given a choice: When the experimenter left the room, the child could either eat one marshmallow or wait until the experimenter returned and be rewarded with two. Long-term studies followed these preschoolers throughout their lives, and they found that the children who waited for the second marshmallow tended to grow up to be more successful adults. Willpower began to be painted as a virtual panacea—the key to all good things in life.

Struck by their findings, the researchers behind the experiment went on to explore the concept of delayed gratification and to answer the questions that were on everyone's minds: Why does willpower succeed or fail in an individual? Why are some people seemingly able to practice it easily while others struggle?

Their research led to a model of the "hot" and "cool" systems to explain why willpower succeeds or fails. The "cool system" is your cognitive and reflective system. This system involves the thoughts about why you should or shouldn't do something. The "hot system" involves your impulses, urges, and primal emotions.

Neurologically speaking, your cool system is your prefrontal cortex. It is where you employ abstract thought and weigh multiple factors to come to a wise decision. The hot system is your primal brain. It involves your amygdala, your hypothalamus, and your hippocampus. It is also where your fight-or-flight response lives. Another (less neurological) way to put it is that your cool system is the angel on one shoulder and the hot system is its devil counterpart on the other. The idea is that willpower fails when your hot system overrides your cool system.

Another classic study that's important to mention is the one about the cookies and the radishes. Back in the late 1980s, a study was conducted in which people walked into a room that smelled like delicious, fresh-baked cookies. In the room was a table with one plate of cookies and one plate of radishes. Some people were told to eat only the cookies (meaning they did not need to exert any willpower) and the others were told to eat only the radishes. Afterward, all the participants had to complete a complex math problem.

As you can imagine, the radish eaters found it hard to resist eating the cookies (requiring the use of willpower for this group), but the cookie eaters didn't need any willpower to resist eating the radishes. The researchers expected to find that the radish eaters (the willpower-depleted group) wouldn't do as well on the math problem, and they were right. The radish eaters gave up on the problem sooner than the cookie eaters did.

The researchers drew the conclusion that willpower is a *depletable resource*. This study sparked follow-up research that also seemed to support this theory. More recently, however, some of the methods used in these experiments have come into question. Although there are likely threads of truth in the theory of willpower depletion, clearly we don't have the whole picture yet, so it is important to stay curious.

While taking this research with the appropriate grain of salt, it remains useful to apply to our everyday lives. Think about all the times and ways you need to exert willpower throughout the day: pulling yourself out of bed when you'd much rather stay tucked in, trying to stay calm in the middle of a distressing conversation, choosing a side salad instead of the onion rings you just saw at the table next to yours. If willpower really is a depletable resource, it's important to be conscious about where you spend your limited supply. One way to do this is to front-load your day by completing the most challenging tasks earlier in the day. If you have trouble getting to the gym after work, for example, then maybe try going to the gym in the morning to maximize the willpower resources available to you to get it done.

Some of the most relevant and exciting current research around willpower comes from the brilliant mind of Kelly McGonigal, PhD, who breaks down the concept of willpower into three separate components: your "I will" power, your "I won't" power, and your "I want" power. The "I will" power pushes you to do something even if it's hard. The "I won't" power is the strength to say no to something that is tempting you. The "I want" power is your connection to your goals and values, and remembering what you really want in the big picture. Each of these powers is associated with different parts of the prefrontal cortex.

Recent research has also identified another not-so-well-known biological factor connected to willpower: heart rate variability. Heart rates typically go up when we're stressed and go down when we're calm. Heart rate *variability* is a measure of the variation of time in between each heartbeat. When it comes to hearts, some variability is a good thing. A healthy heart has tiny variations in the time between beats. Researchers use heart rate variability to measure the level of activation of the fight-or-flight system. When you're stressed, your heart rate increases but the variability decreases, leaving you stuck with feelings of anxiety and anger. When you calm down, your heart rate slows and becomes more variable.

People with higher heart rate variability tend to be better at ignoring distractions, coping with stress, and delaying gratification. But there are many factors that contribute to heart rate variability, including quality of sleep, exercise, and your resting breathing rate. However, it's important to note that heart rate variability can be increased. Some methods involve medical intervention, while others involve behavioral change such as exercise and certain types of meditation. In general, if something activates your cool system, it is likely to be helping increase your heart rate variability and reducing your willpower depletion rate. Mindfulness meditation activates and trains the cool system to be ready for action.

Willpower can also be impacted by your beliefs and attitudes. The reason you're employing willpower impacts how much your willpower is drained. For example, when people feel compelled to do something because they feel they *should* or because they believe other people expect it of them, their willpower resources are more quickly depleted than those driven by internal goals and desires. Have you ever known someone trying to lose weight because they thought they needed to be thinner to be accepted? Compare that approach to someone wanting to lose weight in an effort to give their future selves a gift, imagining a time when they are elderly and still hiking with their grandkids or great-grandkids, for example.

It's also important to point out some disturbing connections between willpower and poverty. The concept of willpower has sometimes conveniently been used by people in power to convince people of lesser means that they are completely responsible for their lot in life, ignoring external factors beyond their control, like socioeconomic background, location, and racial inequities. It can be an easy way for people in power to dismiss the impact of their inherent privilege and to shift the focus away from more important conversations around changing the very structures that support such inequality.

Not only that, but if we continue to peer through this lens and add in the element of willpower depletion, it's easy to see some ways in which people of lesser means are at a real disadvantage. People with more privilege don't have to waste as much willpower on day-to-day decisions about where to spend their money or time. What to have for dinner tonight, for example, becomes only as stressful as identifying what you want and picking up the phone to order it. But for people of lesser means, this means weighing their options much more carefully. People with limited resources have to employ impulse control more often than people with privilege do. Since willpower depletion occurs rapidly during the day, people have little left by the end of the day. Self-control therefore becomes an all-day effort. By the time someone is at the grocery store trying to figure out what to put on the table as cheaply and quickly as possible, they might be a bit more vulnerable to making some unhealthy choices.

There are many other things happening in the big picture other than willpower when it comes to one's ability to make wise choices. For example, behavior is strongly shaped by reward and consequences. We tend to repeat behavior that we're rewarded for and discontinue behavior we're punished for. Children from privileged backgrounds statistically tend to grow up in an environment of reduced chaos and more predictability. Children in this environment learn that waiting is rewarded. Patience is a virtue. Children who grow up with fewer resources, however, are probably rewarded by grabbing what they can when they can get it. It's a reality at many tables that the slowest hand gets the smallest morsel of food.

There's a lot to be learned from the existing willpower research, but it's important to hold it lightly, as much of it can leave us with more questions than answers. We may see that certain factors are related, but we don't know a lot about why that is the case. For the purposes of this book, we'll take what we can learn from the research and identify some tools to gain more self-control and make the most out of your willpower.

BOOST YOUR WILLPOWER

We talked about the prefrontal cortex, the part of your brain behind your forehead that holds many of our special human abilities in this world: abstract thinking, sense of self, and willpower. What if I told you that there is a treatment that will increase the power of your prefrontal cortex and only require 5 to 10 minutes of your time each day and costs you absolutely nothing? Guess what? You've already learned how to do it! Mindfulness meditation is associated with greater gray matter density in your prefrontal cortex. The more you do it, the more this part of your brain grows. Every time you go around the mindfulness clock, from present to distracted to awareness and redirection, you build up this part of your brain, little by little.

Throughout this book you'll discover the ways a mindfulness meditation practice can support and bolster your willpower, paving the way for you to make change more accessible. Not only will this practice build up your prefrontal cortex, but it will also unlock access to all the other proven benefits of mindfulness, from reducing stress to improving immune function. Mindfulness meditation is a foundational practice that covers a lot of ground.

You'll also learn how to improve your ability to focus your attention. Distractibility has been associated with lower self-control. And one doesn't have to look far in this world to find an invitation to be distracted. Our phones are the most obvious example. It seems like these days our attention is our most valuable resource. Everyone wants a piece of it, and advertisers are willing to pay a lot for a moment of our undivided attention. Distractions weigh us down and make it hard to get traction on anything. We'll be looking at tools to help you develop the ability to focus more consistently on the things that matter most to you.

Temptations for instant gratification are everywhere. Our appetite for instant gratification seems endless, and businesses capitalize on this to our disadvantage. Everyone has a desire for instant gratification, but it's important to learn how to approach urges with some hesitation and suspicion. Throughout this book you'll learn how to resist the urge for instant gratification when it works against your larger goals.

We'll also look at the power of habits. Habits, when adapted mindlessly, can plague us. But designing habits intentionally changes the game completely. When you create a new habit, you make it easier to follow through with something. It literally becomes the default. When my clients are looking to start a new habit, I usually encourage them to try to piggyback it onto a habit that already reliably exists in their routine. For example, if you're trying to develop a meditation habit, it tends to be easier if you attach it to something like brushing your teeth or brewing your coffee in the morning. By intentionally creating habits that support the actions you wish to take in life, you reserve your willpower for where you need it most.

Procrastination is one particularly stubborn habit that tends to get in the way of progress. I like the way author and podcaster Gretchen Rubin views procrastination. She describes people as either marathoners or sprinters—either working on something a little at a time until the project is complete, or waiting until the last minute and using the built-up pressure to get things done quickly and efficiently. A marathoner metes out the work. They don't like to work under pressure. A sprinter works best under pressure. Both types of people get things done, just in different ways. The problem comes when a sprinter tries to convince themselves they are a marathoner. They aren't able to enjoy the benefits of experiencing periods of time without pressure; instead, they spend a lot of time beating themselves up for their lack of action until the very last minute when they get it done. It's important to identify which category you most relate to and then use that knowledge to your advantage.

Strong emotions also play a major role in willpower. In addition to influencing how our brain allocates resources, such as redirecting energy away from the prefrontal cortex and to the amygdala when we are in fight-or-flight mode, strong emotions can also cloud our connection to larger goals. When the hot system is activated, it drowns out the cool system. The hot system, being our primal brain, is where we feel the strongest emotions. So in order to apply willpower more consistently and stay on track with our goals, it's important to learn how to navigate strong emotions with awareness. We'll be talking about many ways to do this. It's my goal to show you that Toad can have his cake and his willpower, too.

URGE SURFING

Now that you've learned how to practice mindfulness meditation, let's apply that skill to the experience of impulse control. This practice is called *urge surfing*. The idea is to identify, in a nonjudgmental way, the experience in your body of having an urge to do something but resisting it.

1. Find a relatively quiet place where you won't be interrupted for a bit. Allow your eyes to close and take a few grounding breaths. Try to allow your attention to follow the breath with nonjudgmental awareness. Simply notice how it feels in your body to be breathing moment by moment. Notice when you get distracted and redirect yourself to the breath in the present moment.

2. Next, mentally scan your body for any itches you may be experiencing. Don't try to force anything, but eventually there's usually an urge to scratch somewhere. When this urge comes up, try not to react. Don't move your body. Just take note of where in your body you experience this urge to scratch. Try to notice how that feeling changes moment by moment. Does it stay stable? Does it pulse? Does the itch stay in exactly the same place? Or does it move?

3. Take note of any thoughts that pass through your mind. The first time you try this practice, you might feel like something negative will happen if you resist the urge to scratch the itch. On a visceral level, it could feel a little bit like the urge to scratch is going to balloon until either you scratch the itch or it explodes. Although thoughts like these don't make sense when examined, they can be prominent in your mind in the moment. I invite you to take note of whatever thoughts pass through your awareness and not to make too much of them. Just keep coming back to your experience in the present moment, again and again.

4. Eventually, the urge to scratch the itch will pass. Itches don't last forever, and urges come in waves. The idea behind this practice is that you are *surfing* the wave instead of resisting it. You are noticing how it ebbs and flows over time, resisting the urge to imagine what will happen, instead focusing on cultivating curiosity about your experience one moment at a time.

5. Once the practice is complete, I invite you to try this practice at other times of the day. Notice when you have an urge to do something and pause before reacting, and observe what you can learn from whatever comes up.

KEY TAKEAWAYS

- ▸ Willpower and self-control are complicated concepts that can be broken down into many components.

- ▸ The parts of the brain associated with willpower and self-control are located in the prefrontal cortex, the part of the brain responsible for many of the more highly evolved elements of human functioning.

- ▸ Based on current research, willpower appears to be a depletable resource. However, new research is beginning to challenge that assumption so it's okay to be skeptical and stay current.

- ▸ Self-control can be cultivated to reserve your available willpower, so you can make positive changes in your life.

CHAPTER 3

FINDING FOCUS

Wouldn't it be great if you could focus your attention just as easily as you can focus a camera? What would life be like if you could just choose to focus on something and have your focus remain steady until the task was complete, no matter what happened? In reality, our best efforts to focus our attention can often tumble down a rabbit hole of distractions and leave us wondering what happened.

This chapter will unpack the concept of focusing and look at some of the factors that influence our ability to focus. Most important, it will offer some tools and suggestions to keep your eye on the prize, setting you up for staying focused on what matters.

IN SEARCH OF FOCUS

When successful people are asked about the keys to their success, you often hear the concept of focus emerge. Bill Gates once attributed Steve Jobs's success, in part, to his "ability to focus in on a few things." Inspirational speaker and author Zig Ziglar once said, "I don't care how much power, brilliance, or energy you have. If you don't harness it and focus it on a specific target and hold it there, you're never going to accomplish as much as your ability warrants." The ability to focus is a superpower, but one that is achievable by mere mortal humans. So how did these successful people get it? And how can you get some of it?

How many times have you said, "I just need to focus!" without stopping to think about what focus really is? Is focusing the same as willpower? We tend to use the terms interchangeably, but is that accurate? Although focusing is indeed a part of willpower, it's certainly not the complete picture. The closer you look at the concept of focus, the more it becomes evident how much is unclear. It turns out that focus isn't just about what you're focusing on—it has just as much to do with what you are *filtering out*.

Another way to look at it is to imagine focusing a camera. When you focus a camera, you are adjusting how the camera will interpret the information coming into it. You, as the photographer, get to use the tool of selective focusing to direct viewers' attention at the final image. When you think about it this way, it becomes clear that what you focus on is just as important as what you choose to leave unfocused. Focusing a camera isn't just about turning a knob. You have to adjust your depth of field and fiddle with other settings to decide how much of an area you want to keep in focus. These adjustments have an enormous impact on the final outcome. In the same way, focusing on a task involves many complex facets.

No matter how you look at it, focusing involves, ideally, undivided attention, which can be challenging to cultivate. But when you are fully present with a task, you're able to process information more deeply and engage creative and critical thinking skills. Not only that, but your productivity also soars! However, it isn't as simple as choosing to focus your attention on one thing and having that work. Distractions, both external and internal, are lurking around every corner. Each distraction takes willpower to resist. As we've already discussed, people can easily reach a point of willpower depletion or even exhaustion.

Our attention is often derailed by two separate systems that filter all the sensory input you receive. The first system, called the "automatic system," is always on, monitoring all your sensory input and making automatic decisions for you. This is the part of your brain that tells you to move away from loud noises that hurt your ears or to scream when you feel threatened. It also scans your environment for information you've already decided is relevant or important. In many ways, this is where your habits and primal reflexes are. The second system is the "thinking," or "reflective," system. Any information not handled by the automatic system moves down the line to the reflective system so you can think about it and make a conscious choice about what to do with it.

As you try to focus your attention, you are filtering and processing all kinds of sensory input. Much of it gets filtered out automatically, but some lands on the reflective system's plate, demanding triaging before allowing your attention to refocus on the task at hand. When your phone dings, for example, you have to pause and look at it. You need to process the information enough to decide whether you need to do something about it right then. Then you have to remember what you were originally focusing on and come back to it. All this adds up to making it really hard for our reflective system to remember what you're supposed to be focusing on and to filter out all the background distractions tempting you away from that original goal. Willpower depletion adds up quickly, and focus becomes scarce.

What seems simple on the surface—a plan to focus on a goal until you complete it—becomes much more complicated when you actually try to put it into action. As you try to maintain focus, there's a continual stream of background distractions popping up telling you to focus on other things. Distractions are the enemy of focus. So let's get to know some of the common culprits and learn how to overcome their wily ways.

A WANDERING MIND

The ability to focus our attention on what's most important to us is a deeply valuable life skill. For such an essential skill, though, it can be a hard one to actualize. Sometimes it seems like our minds are programmed to wander instead of focus. It can feel like focusing on one thing at a time is like swimming upstream, as though you're working against powerful forces compelled to push you in the opposite direction. Like the monkey mind we talked about in chapter 1, staying focused on something involves successfully navigating distractions. As if we're playing a video game, we need to keep our eye on the prize while encountering obstacles and challenges on our path. We have to dodge and fight in order to reach our goal—the end of the level—and, hopefully, beat the game. What are some of these obstacles blocking our path?

In his book *Focus: The Hidden Driver of Excellence*, Daniel Goleman, a psychologist who specializes in emotions, makes a distinction between sensory and emotional distractions. Sensory distractions are the external distractions. Emotional distractions are the inner distractions. These emotional distractions are really tough to block out. They tend to be more focused on the negative than the positive. They're hooked into the primal brain, which grabs our attention before we can consciously think about it. Plus, they run on repeat all day, looking for solutions to problems so we can relieve ourselves of the burden of them. But, in reality, this tends to just make matters worse. Goleman writes,

"It's not the chatter of people around us that is the most powerful distractor, but rather the chatter of our own minds." Let's look at both kinds of distractions.

Technology's Role

One of the most common obstacles to our efforts to focus comes from the technology in our lives—our phones, for example. The interactions we have with our screens have an enormous impact on our ability to focus our attention on what really matters to us. One example of this is, of course, notifications. How many times a day does your phone interrupt what you are doing to let you know there's something supposedly more important to attend to?

Not only do we have messages, emails, and phone calls, but we also have apps that we've installed and literally given permission to interrupt us with information like news, reminders, and social media updates. It's easy for our emotions to drive our response to these distractions, especially when the notifications are designed to get us to do just that. News apps, for example, use flashy, "breaking news" headlines to capture the limited attention of readers. The same is true for advertisers, who sprinkle ads throughout our online experience to pull at our heartstrings and give us a sense of urgency. Both are strong foes against our desire to focus.

Outside Interference Plus Internal Noise

In addition to your phone and other devices, there are so many other distractions to contend with throughout your day. Let's take a look at a day in the life of Jesse, for example. Jesse has a big presentation soon. This presentation is for some major stakeholders in the company and could be an opportunity for her to get noticed and finally get promoted. She feels the pressure to put in her best work, but she has tight deadlines to meet and really needs to focus on her presentation. Unfortunately, Jesse works in a cubicle in an open floor office with tons of coworkers who are more than willing to distract her with chats and gossip.

Not only that, but people in cubicles all around her are on their phones all day, and Jesse keeps finding herself unintentionally tracking the conversations she's overhearing. Before refocusing her attention on the task at hand, she admonishes herself in her inner narrative: "Stupid! What are you doing? Don't you know how important this presentation is? You've got to focus!!"

In this example, Jesse was dealing with two different kinds of distractions: external and internal. Externally, she was overhearing conversations that weren't important to her. But her brain was automatically tuned into the human voice and making sense of words. This led to her falling prey to external distractions. But before she was able to refocus, she was distracted by her inner narrative, pausing to punish herself a bit before settling down and refocusing on the task at hand.

Focusing is hard, especially in today's world. But the good news is that focusing is a skill you can practice and strengthen. Next, you'll learn a simple practice to build your ability to focus so that it is ready for you when you need it.

FOCUSED BREATH

Focusing your attention on your breath is harder than it sounds. You breathe all day, every day, without fail. But usually you aren't even aware that you're doing it. It's so easy to forget that every breath is essentially unique. And every breath only happens once. Blink and it's gone.

Why is focusing on the breath so challenging? One reason is that your brain automatically tags it as "boring." That's the automatic system helping you out, letting you focus on other things. But when you intentionally focus on the breath, trying to track it one moment at a time, things get interesting. You are practicing resisting the urge to engage in automatic thought. When you find yourself distracted, you simply bring your attention right back to the breath. You can use this practice anytime you're having trouble focusing. You may find that focusing your attention on even just a couple of breaths can make a big difference.

1. Begin by getting yourself into a comfortable position. You can do this practice while standing or sitting. Lying down can lead to sleeping, though, which would make you miss the purpose of the meditation.

2. Let your eyes close or shift to a soft gaze, not focusing on anything in particular, and gently bring your attention to your breath. There is no need to manipulate your breathing in any way. Notice the experience in your body as the breath comes in and goes out. You may notice the feeling of the air passing through your nose or mouth. You may notice the feeling in your chest as your lungs expand and contract. You may notice all these things or none of these things. Simply allow your attention to track the experience of breathing, one moment at a time.

3. Try to follow the in-breath all the way to the end and the out-breath all the way to the end, just breathing in and out. As your attention goes elsewhere, bring it back to the present moment.

4. To help you focus, you may wish to silently say the word "in" to yourself as you breathe in and "out" as you breathe out. If you find yourself distracted, gently refocus your attention on the breath, picking up wherever you are.

A CALM AND FOCUSED MIND

We've already learned that it's best to conserve your willpower for when it matters most. But focusing your attention on one thing at a time isn't as easy as it sounds. Distractions of all sorts draw you away from the task at hand with magnet-like force. It seems to take constant vigilance to stay focused on what matters most. But, as it turns out, what matters most to you *is* your focus.

The Happiness-Focus Connection

Several years ago, a doctoral candidate at Harvard named Matt Killingsworth conducted a massive research study on happiness. When I say massive, I mean it was huge: His data included 600,000 individual reports from 15,000 people. Participants in this study, which continues to collect data at TrackYourHappiness.org, were prompted by phone at random times throughout the day to answer some quick questions about what they were doing and feeling in that moment. The researchers were hoping to identify the factors most associated with people's happiness. One of Dr. Killingsworth's major findings was that mind-wandering was a strong predictor of unhappiness. (He gave a great TED Talk on this topic. See the Resources section on page 156.) That's right. No matter *what* people were doing, the primary predictor of their happiness was the extent to which they were focused on what they were doing.

This finding means that your ability to stay focused on something is actually quite critical if you care about how happy you are. But as we just talked about, staying focused on something can be tricky business. If Dr. Killingsworth's results are true, and the research is pretty compelling, then we need to practice focusing on what we are doing—whatever it is—if we want to feel happier. It's not about what you do; it's about how focused you are when you do it.

This advice runs contrary to many people's real-life experiences of doing one thing while their minds are elsewhere, like being lost in thought while you're doing the dishes or showering. It's easy to use these times to problem-solve and plan, but what if you could use them to relax and let your mind simply focus on what you are doing in that moment? This brings us to the concept of *unitasking*. If you're slicing a carrot, let yourself just *focus all your attention* on slicing the carrot. Notice the textures and sounds, observing the experience with curiosity and without the need to multitask. We can recharge and practice something that increases our chances of happiness, all while getting things done.

Navigating Choppy Waters

Another way to stack the deck in your favor is to engage in regular practices that help you maintain a calm and focused mind. It's easier to navigate a ship on calm waves rather than choppy waters. You can think of distractions as the wind blowing on these choppy waters: They're going to come and go. What matters is how you respond to them. The better your ability to stay focused on something, the less willpower you'll need to resist the urge to be distracted.

There is a big market for maximizing productivity. In fact, the genre even has a nickname: GTD for "getting things done." There are countless books and articles available espousing tools you can use and techniques you can learn to be more effective at accomplishing tasks. Unfortunately, some of this information amounts to nothing more than additional distractions. However, some of these resources offer valuable tools designed to help people focus their attention in real time, such as identifying priorities and to-do items and keeping track of them in a way that maximizes a person's productivity.

One GTD system that can be especially useful for people trying to make changes in their lives is called bullet journaling, which was developed by Ryder Carroll. This process is popular for people who like to keep track of things in an old-school way: on paper. It involves a daily reflection process of identifying priorities and to-dos, as well as several tools to keep that information organized. I've found this system helpful and shared it with many of my clients, who have also found it useful. It is part of a triaging system that I use to avoid too many distractions when I need to stay focused on something. As potential distractions invade my focus, I use my journal as a bucket to dump all these thoughts in for later consideration. It helps me alleviate the need to take action immediately and allows me to create a space between inspiration and action. Doing so lets me tap into my willpower resources a bit less throughout the day, conserving them for when I really need them.

SEEKING STILLNESS

Maintaining a calm and focused mind can be really challenging when navigating choppy waters. The following meditation practice was written to set you up for success, even when the wind blows. Use this practice whenever you're feeling strong emotions that are making it difficult to stay focused on the big picture.

1. To begin, find a quiet space where you're unlikely to be disturbed for the duration of the practice. Close your eyes. Bring your attention to the present moment with nonjudgmental awareness. Notice when your attention drifts and gently bring it back. Repeat this step again and again.

2. After a few minutes, imagine you are looking at an enormous body of calm water. The body of water is so big that you can see all the way to the horizon, where the water meets the sky. Visualize the surface of the water as smooth and reflecting the boundless sky.

3. Now bring your attention to your body, and notice how it is responding to the imagery. Allow yourself to feel the power of this body of water—its vastness, its incomprehensible size. Experience its stillness as if you were really there. Try to engage all your senses if you can. How would it sound if you were there? Can you imagine the feeling of the ground beneath your feet?

4. Eventually, you will inevitably find your attention drifting. When you find yourself engaged in a thought, imagine it as a small wave in the water, momentarily splashing up and causing a disturbance. Now refocus your attention on the rest of the water. Tap back into that greater stillness. As you do, notice in your peripheral vision the wave calming down and dispersing itself into ripples that get smaller and smaller until they disappear into the rest of the water.

5. Keep bringing your attention back to your experience in the present moment. As you visualize this body of water, how are you experiencing it in your body? Remember, you're just noticing, not making up stories or getting lost in thought or drawing conclusions about anything. You're simply noticing the experience moment by moment. As you gently shift your attention from the visualization of the water back to your internal experience, you're creating a deeper relationship with the stillness embodied by the water.

6. When you are ready, open your eyes and see if you can still hold the feelings in your body. Later in the day, take a moment to close your eyes, take a deep breath, and try to recall the imagery. Notice how your body responds.

THE MINDFUL WAY

One of the most powerful ways you can set yourself up for success—however you define it in achieving the goals you set for yourself—involves your mindfulness meditation practice. You can think of it as *attention resilience training*. You set the intention to focus your attention on the present moment with nonjudgmental awareness. At some point you will naturally get distracted, and when do you do, you gently refocus your attention on where it belongs. Focusing and refocusing your attention builds up your mindfulness meditation practice. The more you practice it, the better you get at it.

And remember, thanks to neuroplasticity, practicing builds up the parts of the brain that you need to resist distractions and stay focused. Every time you notice that you're distracted and you successfully bring your attention back to the present moment, it's like a bicep curl for your prefrontal cortex. As you improve, you'll be able to navigate even more subtle distractions that you might not have noticed otherwise.

As we sit and try to focus on the present moment, we get distracted by external stimuli as well as internal narratives. As we go through the cycle of focusing, getting distracted, and refocusing, we are essentially developing our focusing skills. We are developing our attention resilience skills. And all this increases the chances of calm and steady waters ahead.

In addition, when we engage with mindfulness meditation regularly, our stress and anxiety levels tend to go down, and our sense of well-being tends to increase. This translates into less internal chatter of problem-solving and strategizing, which, as we have seen, generally causes increased stress as opposed to constructive solutions. Reducing our inner distractions paves the way for less choppy waters, which makes it a lot easier for us to stay focused without having to tap too deeply into our valuable willpower reserves.

Remember that your ability to focus is, in many ways, a superpower. When you have undivided attention to offer something that is important to you, amazing things can happen. Bruce Lee once described the "successful warrior" as "the average man, with laser-like focus." Anyone, including *you*, can do extraordinary things with focused attention. The extraordinary inventor Alexander Graham Bell once offered this advice: "Concentrate all your thoughts upon the work at hand. The sun's rays do not burn until brought to a focus." Now that you have the keys to developing your ability to focus, what will you do with your new superpower?

DEFEAT DISTRACTION

A popular tool with my clients is one I teach in my stress management workshops. It was originally made popular by Dwight
Eisenhower, and so it has been dubbed the Eisenhower Matrix.

THE EISENHOWER MATRIX

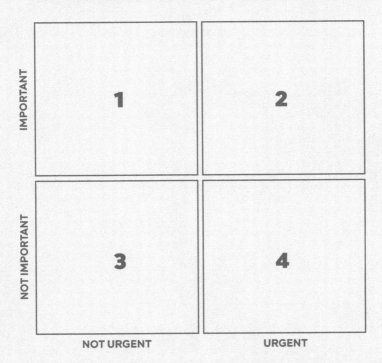

Box 1: These tasks should be scheduled for later.

Box 2: Important and urgent. These tasks should be
the ones you prioritize for action.

Box 3: Not important + not urgent. Eliminate these from
your list. They are unnecessary energy drains.

Box 4: Not important, but urgent. Deligate these tasks to
someone else, if possible.

This simple tool can help you gain perspective on your action items and organize your day a bit more intentionally. This practice will also help you reserve your willpower resources because you are not constantly going back to an overflowing to-do list and repeatedly trying to figure out how to prioritize items.

1. Make a list of all your competing priorities and to-dos.

2. Categorize these tasks based on whether or not they are urgent and important.

3. Plug them all into the matrix.

4. Use your matrix to guide your daily planning and time management. (See Resources on page 156.)

THE POMODORO TECHNIQUE

Humans can only sustain attention for so long. Eventually, our system gets taxed and we experience "hitting a wall." At times like this, no matter how much effort you put into something, you just don't seem to get anywhere. Albert Einstein knew this problem all too well, so he built work-arounds to it into his workday. He was often reported to take breaks from his work to play the violin. Einstein noted how this time helped him reflect on things and generally left him refreshed enough to be able to return to his work with renewed energy and vigor. Elsa, his second wife, once said, "Music helps him when he is thinking about his theories. He goes to his study, comes back, strikes a few chords on the piano, jots something down, returns to his study."

Researchers have often tried to identify a "golden ratio" between focused attention and taking a break to achieve maximum productivity. The popular Pomodoro Technique, created by Francesco Cirillo, is one example of a tool based on this concept. My clients often cite this technique as a useful tool in helping them stay focused on difficult tasks for sustained periods of time. (The name *pomodoro* comes from the Italian word for *tomato* because Cirillo used his kitchen timer, which was in the shape of a tomato.)

1. Choose a task you want to accomplish.

2. Have a piece of paper and something to write with handy.

3. Set a timer for 25 minutes.

4. Begin working on your task and commit to resisting the urge to follow any distractions for those 25 minutes. Everything else can wait—checking your email or phone notifications, getting up to get a glass of water, or anything else—until the timer goes off.

5. When the timer rings, write a check mark on a piece of paper and take a short break of 3 to 5 minutes.

6. Set your timer for this break, and as soon as it goes off, go right back to work on your task for another 25-minute session.

7. Take another short break with your timer set.

8. Repeat this process until you have four check marks on your page.

9. Then take a longer break of 15 to 30 minutes.

10. Repeat the process until your task is complete.

One reason this technique works so well is because it removes the burden of making a choice about where to focus your attention. You are either working or you are on a break. Period. You don't have to stop and focus your attention on a particular distraction and decide whether or not it deserves your attention. The technique allows you to stay focused on what you're doing and minimize any willpower depletion that might otherwise happen. (See Resources on page 156.)

KEY TAKEAWAYS

- Focus is related to, but not equal to, willpower. Focus *is* a major component of how you truly create change and get things done.

- Greater focus is associated with increased happiness. Research indicates that focus is a primary predictor of happiness. Happiness relies less on *what* you are doing, and much more on the extent to which you are *focused* on what you are doing.

- The world has no shortage of obstacles to throw our way in our efforts to stay focused on what is important to us. These obstacles are both external and internal. Developing curiosity and nonjudgmental awareness of these moments of distraction can help you learn from them in order to overcome them.

CHAPTER 4

BREAKING BAD HABITS

How many times have you laid out a plan to do something, only to find at the end of the day you didn't follow through? The best of intentions can crumble in the face of everyday reality. Why is change so hard? One reason is that our behaviors are influenced so deeply by our habits. And habits, by definition, happen when we're not really paying attention to our actions. As we go about our daily lives, our habits carry us through, and we often miss the opportunities for change that pass right underneath our noses. In this chapter, you'll discover why changing habits can be so difficult. You also will learn how to *intentionally create* habits that support your greater intentions. Habits aren't so bad when they're actually helping you make good choices.

BAD HABIT LOOP

Habits are one way our brains try to make the most efficient use of our available resources. It takes a lot of effort to learn and make conscious decisions about things. We would never get anything done if we weren't able to reliably draw on past learning and apply it automatically to current situations.

Consider, for example, learning to drive a car. I remember feeling a great deal of stress as I tried to hold in my mind a list of all the things I needed to remember in each moment to safely drive a car and pass my driver's test. I remember approaching an intersection and needing to run through an enormous checklist in my head: What lane do I need to be in? How much room do I need to leave between the car in front of me and my front bumper? How far away from the traffic light do I need to put on my turn signal? Where are all the mirrors I constantly need to be checking?

It seemed impossible to understand how some people could drive and listen to the radio or carry on a conversation at the same time. But eventually, I started to build habits around my driving. Now I don't need to think about when to switch on my turn signal or how much space needs to be between cars. Driving feels almost instinctual now, but in reality, I've created a series of habits that support my driving skills. My brain has encoded these things for me in such a way that I don't need to tax any of my brain resources to consciously think about them. That leaves valuable resources available for me to think about other things or listen to a podcast.

Most of these habits around driving are examples of good habits. They serve my greater intentions well. Traditionally though, when people talk about habits, they're talking about bad habits. These get the most attention because they cause us the most grief. So let's look a little bit more closely at how bad habits are formed.

When we experience things simultaneously—like a taste (strawberry ice cream!) and a feeling (joy!)—our brain links them through our neurons. There's an old saying in psychology: *Neurons that fire together wire together.* This basically means that our brains hardwire our habits, literally building connective pathways between neurons. This connection is like a super-highway, carrying information between neurons so efficiently that we literally feel a connection between the experiences. So, for example, if you had many positive experiences of eating ice cream when you were younger, you are going to associate ice cream with positive feelings as an adult. This is pleasant, but it also can complicate your relationship with food, as you might start to turn to food to manage your emotions, which tends not to work out very well.

Judson Brewer is a psychiatrist and scientist who studies the power of habits and how to change them. (He has compelling TED Talks worth watching. See the Resources section on page 156.) He uses the term "habit loop" to describe the process of habit formation. A habit loop consists of a trigger, a behavior, and a reward. We experience a *trigger,* which causes us to engage in a *behavior* in response to the trigger, and then we experience something *rewarding* that then increases the chances we will *repeat the behavior.*

Let's see how these three factors contribute to some of the bad habits many of us have developed around the use of our phones. In the days before smartphones were so common, there were many opportunities to pause and be bored. It may sound odd to describe boredom as something positive, but boredom presents a valuable opportunity. During unstructured "boring" time, we can let our minds wander into reflective thoughts, reviewing our experiences and seeing what we can learn from them. Boredom is a mildly unpleasant state, but one that can result in our discovering some original thoughts.

The boredom we would experience while waiting in line or at the bus stop actually used to serve us well. But now, that boredom is quickly remedied with our phones. In this example, the *trigger* is boredom. The *behavior* that comes as a result of the trigger is picking up our phones. You are *rewarded* with a direct hit of dopamine—the "feel good" neurotransmitter that lets you feel pleasure—because someone liked something you said on social media, or at the very least, you distract yourself from the boredom and no longer have to experience it.

Many of us have developed this bad habit of picking up our phones when we're bored, because it brings us the promise of some sense of reward. But the reward we find (if any) is rarely satisfying. Then, when we put down our phones and start to feel bored again, the cycle begins anew. We're strengthening a bad habit, and we're also decreasing our tolerance of the low-level distress boredom provides.

As bad habits go, looking at our phones when we're waiting in line at the store seems harmless enough, but the behavior doesn't usually stop there. Imagine you had an argument with someone you live with. As the dust settles, and you both go into your separate corners, you *might* reflect and learn from the situation. You *might* start to feel pangs of regret and a building awareness of how *you* just may have contributed to the problem. That feeling is inherently uncomfortable. So instead of letting yourself simply experience it long enough to guide you toward corrective action, it's too easy to let yourself get distracted by picking up your phone. That phone helped in other situations where you were feeling uncomfortable, like when you were bored at the grocery store. The longer you stay distracted with your phone, the less likely you are to go back and apologize or reconnect. The distance grows, and you have a new problem on your hands.

BREAKING HABITS ISN'T EASY

Breaking habits is not an easy task. Since habits are automatic, it can be really tricky to notice them when they're happening. Not only that, but we also have built-in systems of reward and past learning to contend with. It can feel like an uphill battle to break bad habits. Research, as well as personal experience, shows us that knowledge alone isn't enough to enact behavioral change. Just *knowing* what you're supposed to do isn't enough to actually make you do it.

Think of your habits and past learning experiences as a sort of scaffolding around your daily life. This scaffolding holds everything else in place. For example, let's look at the habit of brushing teeth. We've been told that brushing teeth twice daily reduces the risk of tooth decay and gum disease. But brushing twice a day, let alone flossing, can be a hard habit to get into. Eventually, though, most of us get into a routine of at least brushing our teeth every evening before we go to bed.

Once this is happening reliably in our routine without our having to consciously think about it, we can trust that this habit will generally continue without too much effort on our part. We don't need to spend any time during the day planning when we will brush our teeth that night. It just happens. It becomes part of the scaffolding surrounding us as we engage with our everyday activities. It supports us and frees us up to do other things. Eventually, it even gives us a place to *hang new habits*, like washing our face after brushing our teeth at night. Once one thing is happening regularly, other habits tend to crop up around it. These habits create the scaffolding that supports the rest of our lives.

But what happens when we want to change our lives? We have to work against the existing scaffolding, and that can be hard. It can feel like everything is working against us. Take, for example, developing a daily meditation practice. Most of the clients I work with want to develop a regular meditation practice of some sort. Once I teach them how to meditate, we come up with a plan for them to practice regularly.

I've never kept track, but I would guess that about 80 percent of the plans clients initially laid out get rejected after the first week. Clients come in with their heads hung low waiting for me to pull out the big red pen and write an "F" somewhere. Instead, they look up to find me smiling. Because we have now learned something we didn't know before about where their best-laid plans can meet their real life. Now we know where to focus our attention and *really* get down to work.

Let's look at one client's plan to meditate after work. She originally told me her plan was to meditate immediately upon returning home from work, before beginning the rest of her evening routine. She woke up every morning with the same plan, but kept finding herself lying in bed that night realizing she had forgotten to do it. The problem was that when she got home from work, she immediately started falling into old habits. Those old habits were like a wave, carrying her through the rest of the evening without giving her a chance to pause and notice that she was forgetting to meditate.

The scaffolding that helped her be efficient with her time in the past was now working against her in the present. We needed to revise her plan to help her raise awareness of the moment when she needed to shift her habitual way of responding to the moment, and instead practice a new habit—to go meditate.

She set herself up for success by placing a sticky note reminder on the wall that she would see when she first walked in her front door. After some time, meditating when she arrived home became a new habit, and she could take down the sticky note because she no longer needed it. The habit was now a part of her scaffolding, making it easier for her to meditate without having to think about it.

For a while, as she was dismantling the old scaffolding and building a new one, her willpower resources were a bit more taxed. As her scaffolding was "under construction," she couldn't rely on her automatic patterns as much as she used to. She needed to slow down and think more consciously about her actions in the present moment long enough to intentionally build a new scaffolding. At the same time, she had to continually resist the urge of reinforcing her old scaffolding. But eventually, the new scaffolding took hold, and her meditation practice no longer required much in the way of willpower to keep going.

Our habit loops create our scaffolding. And habit loops have many different kinds of triggers. Some of the triggers are environmental. For example, when we see the candy bowl on the counter, we're triggered to grab some candy. Other triggers are less visible, such as our thought habits. When we're feeling sad, we might tell ourselves to drown our sorrows in a package of cookies. It's vitally important to stay curious to identify triggers and associations you might not be fully aware of. Your mindfulness practice can help you bring awareness to the scaffoldings that are supporting, or hindering, your success.

NOTICING ASSOCIATIONS

Sometimes, we can develop habits and associations with certain rooms in our homes. For example, some of my clients feel an automatic sense of dread whenever they walk into the bathroom and look in the mirror. By bringing awareness to this unconscious habit, they are able to pause for a moment before they walk into the bathroom and intentionally counter this feeling by practicing self-compassion. But the first step is learning to notice what feelings might come up for us. The following practice offers you the opportunity to dig in and get curious about your relationship to the spaces in your home, and to shine a light on the hidden forces (thought habits and felt memories) impacting your ability to change your habits. You can apply this practice to any location you have an association with, such as work or school, to increase your awareness of how these environments impact you.

1. Start in any room in your home. Find a place to sit for a few minutes and let your body relax. Close your eyes but keep the image of the room in your mind's eye as you take some slow deep breaths and bring your attention to your body.

2. Follow your experience of the breath for a few moments. Simply observe how it feels to have the air entering and leaving your body one moment at a time.

3. When you find your mind wandering, gently redirect your attention to your body in the present moment.

4. Now, open your eyes briefly and remind yourself what room you are in. Glance around and observe your reactions to what you see. There is no need to judge, and I encourage you to resist the urge to problem-solve anything. Try not to worry about interpreting what you feel. Simply notice what comes up for you, whether it's clear feelings or simply sensations.

5. Allow your eyes to close again as you observe the feelings you are left with. What did you notice?

6. Now, open your eyes and relocate yourself to another room. Any room will do, but ideally you are choosing rooms where you engage in your habits, like the bathroom, kitchen, bedroom, or living room. Repeat the same process of observing whatever comes up for you as you enter the room and look around.

Over the next few days, I invite you to periodically pause and take a breath when you enter a room and observe your reactions. These reactions are part of the scaffolding that you encounter when trying to change the habits you engage in every day. I recommend you take some time to write out some thoughts about what you noticed.

CULTIVATING HEALTHY HABITS

As stated earlier in the chapter, one of the reasons habits are so tricky to change is that, by definition, they happen when we're not paying attention. Habits are, in many ways, our default mode. They are the directions we gravitate toward when we aren't specifically focusing our attention on any particular thing. Habits serve us well . . . until they don't.

In order to change habits, we need to be present enough to notice when they are happening and then identify alternative responses. *All change happens in the present moment.* If we want to make changes, it makes sense to start there. The thing is, though, being fully present can be challenging. As we've already discovered with our basic mindfulness meditation practice, staying present is no easy task.

I remember working with a client on weight loss. Despite the fact that my client seemed to be doing all the things she needed to do to lose weight, she still couldn't change the number on the scale. We figured there was something happening underneath the surface, and we suspected it had to do with some automatic behavior. I asked her to practice keeping a food log to track everything she ate and how she felt when she ate it. This led her to realize that her stress level was getting higher in the evenings, and she was managing these emotions by nibbling on food while she prepared dinner. These "hidden calories" had a close relationship to her emotions. Bringing awareness to this habit helped her change it.

Another challenge is that sometimes when we pause and really pay attention, we don't like what we see. Sometimes under the surface you'll uncover unpleasant and unhelpful narratives within you that are driving your habits. I can't overstate the importance of practicing self-compassion during this process. (For more information about how to develop more self-compassion, see Kristen Neff and Christopher Germer's program and workbook, included in the Resources section on page 156.) By practicing a nonjudgmental stance, you optimize your ability to make use of the information that comes up. You're able to lower your defenses enough to relax and get curious enough to allow yourself to *really* learn from the present moment.

One of the worst bad habits that stops many, if not most, people from growth is *self-judgment*, which can translate into the fear of saying the wrong thing or stepping on someone's toes. This fear can turn into inaction and then worse, into feelings of shame. Why the fear? All learning starts with a simple awareness of a gap in your knowledge. This awareness gives you the opportunity to learn from your experience and set yourself up for success next time. But too often people fall into the trap of focusing on self-shame, and they replay the event in their head on repeat and revive a feeling of embarrassment over and over again.

Why do we punish ourselves? It's such a waste of time and energy! Mindfulness lets you become present enough to *get curious* about your reactions, and to turn them into more *conscious, intentional responses.*

Another client I worked with a few years ago found that she was avoiding going to the gym because of the negative self-talk she found accompanying her visits to the locker room. As she applied mindful awareness to the act of viewing herself in the mirror, she was able to identify a self-judgmental narrative that had been there all along. She was able to connect this to some stressful and embarrassing memories in her school locker room many years prior. Applying self-compassion intentionally in these moments, allowed her to experience less resistance to going to the gym.

Remember that as you practice new habits, your brain's neuroplasticity is engaged. You develop new habits and default modes, but ones you *intentionally choose to create*. How do you practice habit change? Let's walk through an exercise designed to do just that.

DEPRIORITIZING YOUR PHONE

Many of us have developed questionable habits related to our phones. We've developed mindless, automatic ways of reacting to our phones that may or may not actually serve us well. With this practice, you will visualize a healthier relationship with your phone and pave the way for new, more intentional habits with it.

1. To prepare, I recommend you either set your phone to interrupt you with a notification or ask a friend to text you randomly during the period of time you set aside for the practice. (I suggest 5 to 10 minutes.) Be sure your phone notifications are on. Set your phone down near you, facedown, and make sure you're not touching it.

2. Begin with a basic mindfulness practice. Take a few moments with your eyes closed to reacquaint yourself with the present moment through your senses. Notice when you get distracted by thoughts and gently refocus your attention on the present moment without judgment.

3. Bring into your mind's eye the room around you and specifically the phone next to you. Try to imagine looking at it. Notice your body's responses. Does your heartbeat change? Do you notice any urges to reach out to it? Try to just observe and listen to your body's responses. If you don't notice anything, don't worry about it. Just keep listening.

4. Notice how your impulses ebb and flow during the practice. Notice the direction of your thoughts. Try not to get too caught up in the thoughts. Just take note and then come back to the present moment.

5. Imagine the phone making a sound. Imagine feeling strong in your desire to not be distracted by it. Try to imagine yourself sitting in awareness that your phone has made a noise, but you are choosing to not respond. Notice how that feels in your body.

6. When your phone makes a sound, resist the urge to open your eyes. Try to drop in and get curious about your body's reactions to the notification. Try to practice nonjudgmental awareness. Just observe. Notice when your mind wanders, perhaps to wondering whether you should stop meditating to check your phone. If that happens, just remind yourself you can most likely be offline for these few minutes. Just practice riding it out.

7. Toward the end of the meditation time, open your eyes and look at the phone, but do not turn it over or touch it. Notice any changes in your body and thoughts. Does the desire to check it increase? Decrease? How do you experience it in your body *in this moment*?

8. When you're ready, make an intentional decision to slowly look at your phone without reaching for it. Pause before reaching for it. Continue noticing your body's responses.

9. Throughout the rest of the day, try to build in a mindful pause as an automatic habit in response to your phone notifications. With intentional pausing, taking a breath, and identifying how you wish to respond, you are creating a new relationship with your phone. You may wish to support the practice by changing the tone on your phone to a bell to remind you to pause and breathe before reaching for it.

THE MINDFUL WAY

During the day, our scaffoldings support us through a dizzying number of complex reactions and habits that run with little or no awareness on our part. If we want to get from one side of the room to the other, for example, it seems like we just think about it and we are there. But in reality, we had to learn how to make all the connections between our muscles and our thoughts and our senses to learn a complex behavior like walking. This is why it takes children a long time to master this skill. The behavior itself is quite complicated. We rely on our ability to enact these processes automatically so we can focus our attention on other things while we're doing it. And focus on other things *we do*. Our monkey minds leap into action and bounce from tree to tree. We don't even notice what it takes to get our bodies to move through space.

Usually we want our scaffolding to be in the background, without our awareness. But this works against us when we are trying to make changes to it. Our task is to bring awareness to the habits that support the behaviors we want to change so we can recognize the opportunities in each moment to try something new. Mindfulness meditation, in many ways, is the act of pulling back the curtain and injecting curiosity into our everyday habits so we can recognize the opportunities for change that exist in each moment.

We all have pockets of time that occur on a regular basis when we don't have to consciously be thinking about what we're doing so our minds can focus on other things. Taking a shower, driving to work, washing dishes—these are all things we can pretty much do on autopilot. That leaves our monkey minds free to explore. Our troop of monkeys tends to gravitate toward certain neighborhoods and some of them are better than others.

I briefly referred to *windshield wiper* practices in chapter 1. These are practices of bringing mindful awareness to everyday activities. Washing dishes is one example. I used to find my mind wandering while washing dishes every night. My thoughts would gravitate toward problem-solving and, if left unchecked, worrying. I started to recognize that these thoughts left me feeling resentful and frustrated after the dishes were done, and eventually, I started practicing mindfulness instead. While washing dishes, I would periodically refocus my attention on the present moment by noticing my experiences without judgment. I would observe the feel of the water flowing through my hands. I would try to focus on just one dish at a time, resisting the urge to judge the experience or let my attention drift to something else.

These windshield wiper practices can help you keep your lens clean so you can more clearly and directly interact with each moment. By "lens," I mean your ability to see and experience things. A clear lens is better than one that is primed to interpret everything negatively. Instead of smudging your lens with feelings of resentment and frustration from thought patterns that might happen to pop into your mind, you are left feeling more energized and curious about what the next moment will bring. This kind of attitude paves the way to injecting new responses to old habits and behaviors. It helps you recognize and make the most of the opportunity in each moment.

You can think of windshield wiper practices as a kind of informal mindfulness practice, one that draws from the well you have filled with your regular formal mindfulness meditation practice. Formal practices and informal practices work together to help you get the most out of your meditation routine. Let's look at a couple of other practices that have both a formal and informal component you can experiment with to bring awareness to your everyday habits, thus offering you real opportunity to change the way you respond to them.

MINDFUL EATING

We tend to be disconnected from our actual experience of eating. Practicing mindful eating is one way to reconnect your attention to the present moment through fully immersing yourself in the experience of eating. Mindful eating, when practiced regularly, has been associated with many positive outcomes, including achieving (and maintaining) a healthy weight. Plus, if you enjoy eating something, why not truly allow yourself to slow down and focus all your attention on the experience? Let's give it a try. Before we begin, I suggest you get something to eat. It doesn't need to be much, just a bite or two of some food.

1. Begin by letting your eyes close and taking a few grounding breaths. Reacquaint yourself with the present moment through your senses. Practice focusing and refocusing your attention with open awareness on the present moment.

2. Open your eyes and look at the food in front of you. Try to look at it as if it's the first time you've ever encountered this particular kind of food. Try to tap into a sense of curiosity about it. Notice any reactions that come up. Observe them as they pass through your awareness, resisting the urge to make much of any of them. Just keep coming back to witness the experience, with no other agenda.

3. Reach out and pick up the piece of food. Place it under your nose and smell it, allowing your eyes to close so you can focus completely on how it smells. Open your eyes again and look at it from a different angle. Notice the textures and shapes and shadows. Notice any thoughts as they come up, but don't let yourself get too distracted by them.

4. Now place the food in your mouth but resist the urge to chew it automatically. If you feel the urge to chew, simply bring awareness to the experience. How do you feel the urge? Can you locate where in your body you feel it? Does the experience change over time? Don't rush through this step. A lot can be learned if you sit back and deeply explore with all your senses.

5. Allow yourself to take a bite and notice how your experience changes. How has the flavor changed? The texture? How has the urge to chew shifted now that you have chewed the food one time? Resist the urge to think too much about it. Simply notice and keep noticing.

6. Now, allow yourself to continue chewing and observing how your experience evolves. At what point do you experience the most flavor? When does the texture fully break down? When you notice the urge to swallow, simply observe it before giving in to it, noticing the experience of swallowing.

7. Once you have swallowed and your bite is complete, try to bring curiosity to your body's reactions to it. How far down your throat can you still feel the food? At what point can you not feel it anymore? How is the rest of your body reacting to that bite of food? Allow yourself to learn from this moment before moving on to the next bite.

A formal mindful eating practice sets the stage for changing your relationship with food. But it is unlikely you have the time or desire to practice mindful eating every time you eat. One popular informal practice that can be powerful is to bring mindful awareness to your *first and last bites* of food each day, or of each meal. As you bring intentionality to the opening and closing of your eating experience, you set up a framework of intentionality that supports the eating that happens between.

MINDFUL LISTENING

Mindful listening is another practice that can have a deeply positive impact on your efforts to change habits, specifically your habits in relation to the people in your daily life. We all fall into habits of thinking about other things when we're trying to listen to someone or something. Our minds quickly get bored, and we assume we've heard all that we need to hear, quickly moving on to other things. Have you ever been introduced to someone and then you immediately forgot their name? We are often multitasking, trying to identify the next thing we are going to say which, in turn, limits our ability to *actually hear* what is being said. A formal mindful listening practice helps us get better at attending to what we are hearing, which will make it easier to listen more carefully when we want to.

1. To begin, I recommend you go outside, if that is an option for you. Listening to sounds outdoors is a different experience from listening to the sounds in our homes. Although it is certainly possible to practice mindful listening at home, it tends to be more enjoyable and easier to practice outdoors. I also recommend you set a timer so you don't need to worry about keeping track of time.

2. Begin by closing your eyes and focusing your attention on the sounds you hear. Try to resist the urge to label the sounds or identify what is making them. Try to simply observe the sounds as sounds themselves. Notice the qualities of the different sounds and how they evolve moment by moment. Try to resist the urge to judge or interpret what you hear or think. Simply let your attention track the sensory input coming through your eardrums in each moment.

3. Notice when your mind wanders. Inevitably, you will find yourself thinking about other things. When that happens, try not to judge. Simply bring your attention right back to the

sounds in the present moment and continue listening with open, nonjudgmental awareness.

4. You might notice that what you initially assume to be "silent" often has rich, albeit subtle, sounds within it. We rarely experience true and complete silence. If you find your mind deciding that there is nothing to notice, keep listening and see what emerges. You may find the experience deepens, like when your eyes adjust to the dark when you go stargazing. What initially seems like empty sky eventually reveals a breathtaking number of pinpoints of light that previously had been invisible to your eye. The soundscape reveals itself with stillness and patience. Your job is to practice deep listening.

The more you practice mindful listening, the more you'll be able to leverage that skill when you're interacting with other people. An informal mindful listening practice can involve intentionally offering your undivided attention to conversations for a few moments (or longer). Resist the urge to come up with the next thing you're going to say. Resist the urge to worry about the other person's reactions to you. Simply offer the other person your undivided attention for a few moments and just keep bringing your attention back when it wanders away.

KEY TAKEAWAYS

- Habits, by definition, happen automatically. Don't underestimate their power. They can either help or hinder us in our efforts to change our behavior in very real ways.

- Habits are created through habit loops. Habit loops are a way to describe the relationships between a *trigger*, which prompts a *behavior*, which then accesses a *reward*, which increases the likelihood of repeating the loop.

- Breaking habits is easier said than done. But there are ways to set yourself up for success.

- Mindfulness meditation is your most powerful tool to bring awareness to old habits and intentionally create new ones that support your greater goals.

CHAPTER 5

CONQUERING PROCRASTINATION

No matter how well we've planned ahead, sometimes when it really comes down to it, we make other choices. Have you ever made a plan to do something, like go to the gym first thing in the morning only to wake up with less motivation? Have you ever found yourself saying, "I can always do that later, or tomorrow," and then after a week or so, wonder what happened? Procrastination happens to everyone, despite the fact that it often gets in the way of our hopes and dreams.

Mindfulness is the most effective tool I have found to combat the habit of procrastination. This chapter will explain some of the reasons we procrastinate as well as some of the reasons that account for why it's so hard to stop this particular habit. We'll also talk about why mindfulness is so useful in the fight against procrastination. And we'll explore some exercises to aid you in your efforts to overcome this habit.

PROMISING AND POSTPONING

Procrastination is essentially a cycle of promising and postponing that disguises itself as progress, but in reality is stagnation. That stagnation is often accompanied with unpleasant emotions like shame, frustration, and hopelessness. You promised to do something, but then ended up choosing to do something else. Why would you do such a thing? Doesn't it strike you as highly illogical? In fact, this issue has plagued humanity for centuries, if not millennia. The ancient Greek philosophers even made a word for it: *akrasia*, which means "the state of acting against your better judgment through weakness or will." So why does it happen? Let's look a bit more deeply into this.

We briefly looked at author Gretchen Rubin's distinction between "marathoners" and "sprinters" in chapter 2. We all know people who fit into these categories. If you recall, the *marathoners* are people who break a big project down into manageable chunks, working on it a little at a time so that it is ready before the deadline. The *sprinters*, however, intentionally wait until the deadline is near before they start working because they know they work best under pressure. There is nothing inherently right or wrong about either of these approaches. They're both the right approach for the right person.

Procrastinators are often sprinters who wish they could, or feel like they "should," be more of a marathoner. They tend to judge themselves for not acting like a marathoner, causing them to lose the benefit of rest and recovery time the sprinter usually benefits from when they *intentionally* choose to delay action. When the deadline approaches for a sprinter, they find the energy required to get it done without it taking too much of a toll on them. When the procrastinator approaches the deadline, however, they are already exhausted.

For many people, procrastination is a habit they fell into because of their difficulty with processing strong emotions and regulating them in a healthy way. Let's take, for example, a client I worked with recently who was trying to be more successful with his weight loss efforts. For the sake of this discussion, we'll call him Mateo. One key habit for weight loss involves the task of keeping a food log. This means keeping track of everything you eat when you are eating it, and I usually ask clients to start one right away. However, despite agreeing that it is a good idea, many people resist actually keeping a food log. Mateo was no exception. It took a long time for him to develop a food-logging habit.

Although it's kind of a pain in the neck to drag a notebook around and remember to write in it all day, this isn't usually the reason people don't do it. When we would talk about why he hadn't completed his food log, Mateo would mumble excuses about logistics, like it was a bad week to start tracking because of his schedule, or he needed to buy a new notebook.

Eventually, though, we were able to identify that whenever he even thought about writing in the food log, he felt gripped by anxiety. The more he thought about the food log, the larger the emotional response would get. Ultimately, Mateo developed a strong negative association with the idea of food-logging, so whenever he approached the task, he became overwhelmed by negative feelings.

After he learned distress-tolerance skills and emotion-regulation skills (more on those later), Mateo was able to pave the way for himself to finally get on with the task of writing in his log. This wasn't easy, of course. It took work and courage for him to be willing to sit with those big feelings and find ways to self-regulate. Eventually, the fear was replaced with a sense of self-confidence that he could approach tasks effectively, even when the tasks felt scary or impossible at the time.

Another way to look at what happened with Mateo is that his automatic system tagged food-logging as something that should trigger his fight-or-flight response. When you experience fight-or-flight, a natural response is to flee the situation. When the situation is actually a task you want to complete, one way to "flee" the situation is to do something that distracts you and feels good in the moment: You eat some food, look at your phone, or watch some TV. You get rewarded because you're no longer feeling the negative emotional response to the task you avoided. ("I don't have to log food now. Whew!") But that reward is short-lived when you realize you've just wasted time not doing the thing you intended to do. ("Another day where I failed to log my food.") This can trigger negative self-talk and the negative emotional states that come with it, making the negative association with the task even worse.

RESISTING THE URGE

Once it gets started, procrastination can be a really tough habit to break. It seems like there's a lot working against you when you try to stop procrastinating. Let's take a closer look at some of the hidden factors contributing to the challenge of breaking the procrastination habit.

Have you ever tried to save up for something that you really wanted? If so, you probably know the lure of impulse spending. No matter how much you may want that future reward, the fact is that we humans tend to value immediate rewards more highly than future ones. So those impulse purchases can suddenly seem much more attractive than the vague idea of saving up for the larger goal down the line. In other words, when we really break down the process we go through when making decisions about what to do next, our brains tend to miscalculate the value of short-term gains versus long-term rewards. The short-term relief promised by distraction feels more powerful in the moment than the long-term reward of following through with the task, even though it would unlock the truly more rewarding goal of successfully completing the task. It's harder to feel in any real or tangible way the potential value of a future reward.

We also have the problem of task-avoidance. When we think about doing the thing that tempts us to procrastinate, we tend to focus on the worst parts of the task. Then we categorize everything related to that task in the same bucket—"scary" or "overwhelming"—when in reality, the majority of the tasks may be relatively neutral. This means that the worst part of the task you are avoiding expands in your mind and seems to represent the entire task. For example, you may avoid cleaning the garage because you know you have a box in there with mementos that will trigger grief and memories of someone you lost recently. You might focus so much on how hard it will be to go through that box that you forget 99 percent of the garage is filled with stuff that is much easier to organize and sort through.

In addition, when you experience anxiety associated with task-avoidance, it can escalate to the point of activating your fight-or-flight system. As we discussed previously, when your fight-or-flight system kicks in, your brain tends to allocate resources away from your prefrontal cortex—your thinking brain—in order to deal with the crisis that the fight-or-flight system has identified. This makes it even harder to access the parts of your brain associated with decision-making and long-term goals.

Today's world offers us an endless stream of distractions that tempt us with the promise of instant gratification. One way these distractions get in our way is that they offer a tempting escape from whatever task we don't want to do. Whether we're talking about video games, our electronic devices, or grabbing a tempting snack of convenience food, opportunities for distractions surround us. In moments when we're tempted to procrastinate, these distractions make it really easy to do so.

Multitasking is another way to invite procrastination. It can seem like the best way to be efficient is to have multiple pots on the stove simmering at once, as you jump from task to task. In reality, though, you waste so much time jumping from task to task and refocusing your attention on each task that it can actually backfire and make you much less productive overall. It's easy to see how the monkey mind can take over, making it increasingly difficult to focus on any one thing for long enough to feel a sense of completion. It is almost like training to be really good at procrastination down the line. If you're not feeling immediate satisfaction for completing something, it's tempting to just switch gears and focus on something else. Once you get on a roll, it's hard to stop.

After reading all this information, it might seem like resisting the urge to procrastinate is a lofty goal, better left to tomorrow. (See what I did there?) I'm here to tell you to not believe it! Just because the deck is stacked against us in some ways, that doesn't mean we can't still pull off a winning hand. The first step is being aware of what's really happening.

It's hard to build awareness of what's happening in the moment without practicing staying in the moment long enough to access that information. It is challenging to try to keep your attention focused on one thing at a time. And it can be jarring to track your attention as it jumps anywhere it can to avoid focusing on the one thing you're trying to do. One way to build your chops in this area is to practice focusing on the breath. Breathing is a fine example of something your brain wants to classify as boring; your brain can do it automatically. You don't really need to focus on it. But resisting the urge to let your mind wander from it means practicing the very skills you need to defeat procrastination elsewhere in your life. So give it a try.

UNITASKING

Unitasking is the practice of simply doing one thing at a time. For this meditation, your one task will be to focus on your experience of breathing in the present moment. Just like in previous meditation practices, you will track the experience of the breath in the present moment with nonjudgmental awareness, noticing when you get distracted and gently bringing yourself back. But in this meditation your task is to count your breaths, simply noticing the increase in number and counting them one at a time. As you will soon find, this practice can be surprisingly challenging.

1. Begin by settling your body into a comfortable position. I encourage you to find a stance that feels relaxing but that also invites alertness. Sitting up or standing is generally a wise choice.

2. Allow your eyes to close, and focus your attention on the present moment. Bring your attention to your body and notice how your body responds to the act of breathing, moment by moment. Remember to scan your whole body. You may be surprised with what you find. You may notice your clothing shifting as your chest rises and falls, for example. Try to treat each breath as its own experience, noticing any subtle differences in your experience from one moment to the next.

3. Practice observing the breath for a few minutes. Notice when your mind wanders and gently bring it right back to the present moment with nonjudgmental awareness. If it feels comfortable to do so, allow your breathing to slow down and deepen.

4. Next, I invite you to begin counting your breaths. As you breathe in, say the word "one" to yourself. As you breathe out, say "one" again. Then, as you breathe in again, say the word "two," and as you breathe out, say the word "two" again in your head.

5. Continue in this way until you lose track of what breath you are on. When you lose track, reset the counter to one. Try to resist the urge to judge your progress. You are counting the breaths, not judging your ability to count the breaths. Simply notice what happens and resist the urge to get lost in judgmental thoughts.

AN ATTENTIVE MIND

Learning to tame your own unique version of the monkey mind can be an essential tool in combating the urge to procrastinate. Earlier in this chapter, I hinted at procrastination essentially being an emotion regulation or distress tolerance problem. Your troop of mental monkeys (aka "monkey mind") has a great deal to do with these problems as they drag your attention around with them. So the ability to tame these monkeys in the moment is an essential element of self-control.

Let's imagine for a moment a tree with a pack of monkeys sitting in it. Monkeys are excitable creatures, and this group is no exception. They're all poised, ready to act the moment anyone calls an alarm. When any one of them senses danger, they start to screech. Almost immediately, the rest of the pack springs into action, calling out in response with increasing intensity. They start jumping from limb to limb, looking around and trying to figure out what's going on. Suddenly, a tiger appears through the underbrush, the screeching comes to a climax, and the monkeys scatter with dizzying speed.

Now imagine yourself approaching a task that you've been avoiding. Perhaps you feel tense, almost as if you're prepping for battle. Unpleasant emotions start building. Perhaps you push yourself with a poorly designed pep talk, telling yourself, "Get off your butt and make this happen this time. Look at all your failures in the past! Don't let that be now!" As you approach the task, your emotional activation increases, and your flight-or-flight system gets the signal, readying itself to activate.

Your pack of monkeys senses that something is up. They are ready to pounce into action at a moment's notice. Depending on how you approach the next few moments, those monkeys might scatter, taking with them your valuable attention—attention that you need in order to follow through on the task. So it makes sense to arm yourself with the valuable information about how to keep those monkeys as calm as possible. And in the moments when they get excited or even scatter, you want to know how to quickly tame them and bring them back to where they belong.

Some essential skills to tame our monkey minds involve *tolerating emotional distress* (which doesn't mean you have to like or agree with what is distressing you) and the ability to *regulate your emotions*, which means modulating your response to the trigger so you can *respond*, rather than *react* in habitual ways. I've dedicated a whole chapter later in this book to emotion regulation, so let's talk here about how to tolerate emotional distress.

One of the best ways to tolerate emotional distress experienced in the present moment is to simply focus on your senses. A spark of emotion can quickly be whipped up into a roaring flame with the help of our inner narratives, our thoughts. Our thoughts are never really in the present moment. They are generally about the past or the future, or they're analyzing what's happening in the present moment. Your senses, however, are always the doorway to the present moment. By focusing your attention on your senses, instead of on your thoughts, you stop fanning the flames and give those embers a chance to die down.

SETTLING THE MONKEYS

This informal mindfulness practice gives you a quick and easy way to return to the present when you're experiencing emotional duress.

1. Close your eyes and take a few grounding breaths. Allow your attention to track your experience of the breath, moment by moment.

2. Now bring your attention to your sense of sound. Notice whatever sounds are happening around you, big and small. Try to listen to the silence with as much interest as you listen to familiar noises.

3. Try to resist the urge to label or analyze the experiences. Simply note them as facts, without judgment. When you're observing sounds, for example, try to stick to observing sounds as a soundscape. It's like focusing on a landscape as opposed to an individual building within it. You're not focusing on any one particular sound or trying to identify where it came from. You're trying to simply observe the sounds themselves for a little bit.

4. Continue by applying the same process through each of your senses (sound, touch, sight, smell, and taste). After a little while, you will notice your emotions have calmed down a bit and your monkeys are at ease again.

Naming emotions as they are experienced is associated with the ability to tolerate emotional distress. This is easier said than done, though, because emotions can be difficult to identify in the moment and are rarely (if ever) experienced in isolation. Emotional experiences are complex, and it's easy to get swept away by them. The following applied mindfulness practice is designed to practice naming your emotions without getting overly distracted by them. This is a useful skill when trying to tolerate emotional distress. Because avoiding emotional distress is a prime contributor to procrastination, this practice can be a useful tool to defeat the habit.

WHERE DOES YOUR MIND GO?

If you have tried any of the meditation practices that I've shared with you so far in this book, you have discovered how difficult simply keeping your attention in the present moment can truly be. So far in our practices, you've focused on developing the ability to refocus your attention on the present moment. Now you're going to build on those skills to hold your attention in the present moment long enough to name your distractions without getting too caught up in them.

Where does your mind go? This practice was designed to help you answer that question. You may want a pen and paper to take a few notes when you're done.

1. To begin, sit in whatever position you normally use to meditate. Allow your body to rest in a relaxed but alert position. Allow your eyes to close and allow your attention to follow the breath. Try to simply observe your experience of the breath, one moment at a time.

2. As your mind wanders, try to notice and label the distractions. Were you focusing on a feeling? If so, what feeling? Were you engaging in a narrative? What's the easiest way to categorize that narrative? Worrying? Planning? Judging? Analyzing? Daydreaming?

3. Once you label the distraction, try to leave it at that. Resist the urge to engage in a debate about the distraction or its importance. Try not to judge the distraction. Simply notice it and then refocus your attention on the present moment, just like you would deal with any other distraction during a regular mindfulness meditation practice.

4. Once you're finished with your practice, take a moment to note any trends you experienced, such as spending much of your time worrying or engaging in negative self-talk. It may be helpful to write down anything useful that you learn from the experience and to refer to it again when you practice this in the future. You may start to notice long-term trends that are worth addressing.

THE MINDFUL WAY

Why is mindfulness so useful for helping us focus and overcome the nasty habit of procrastination? We've already looked at the value of mindfulness in helping us name our emotions. We've also used mindfulness as a way to focus on the breath through our counting meditation. Now let's look more closely into some of the ways a mindfulness meditation practice can powerfully assist you in your efforts to overcome procrastination.

As you recall from chapter 1, mindfulness meditation engages the brain's neuroplasticity, which impacts how the brain works in specific and relatively consistent ways. One of the predictable ways this happens is that your brain reallocates resources toward your prefrontal cortex and builds up more brain material there (otherwise known as gray matter). This is the part of the brain responsible for *executive functioning*, the ability to be effective at decision-making, impulse control, and abstract thought. These are the very skills that we need to overcome procrastination. Just by engaging in a regular mindfulness meditation practice, you are building your executive functioning skills.

Mindfulness meditation can, in many ways, be seen as "strength training" for this part of the brain. The brain responds to your mindfulness practice by building up more gray matter density in that area and also developing more connections between that part and the rest of the brain. At the same time, gray matter density in the amygdala (the very part of the brain we are trying to quiet down; the home of fight-or-flight) decreases. The number of connections between the amygdala and the rest of the brain decreases as well, all through the practices offered in this chapter. But we aren't done yet: I have two more meditations for you to try.

Changing procrastination habits takes a lot of self-awareness. We tend to go about our days lost in thoughts and relying on our habits to carry us through our daily routines. It takes a lot of awareness to pause and recognize the opportunity for change that comes with every moment. It's amazing how revolutionary it can feel to access the present moment through mindful awareness. Often likened to "child's mind," mindful awareness is a way for you to view each moment with a sense of curiosity. It reduces the effectiveness of mindless, automatic reactions. Mindful awareness also helps you "clean your lens" and see more clearly what your options are in each moment and gives you the ability to access new ways of responding instead of reacting.

NOTICING THE URGE TO PROCRASTINATE

This meditation is the first "off-the-cushion" practice introduced in this book. As such, this practice may be the most challenging one you've encountered so far. It involves noticing the urge to procrastinate as it comes up *in real life*. Instead of scheduling this practice on your own time, this is a practice that you need to apply in the moments you experience the urge to procrastinate. So your approach to it needs to be a little different from how you handled the other practices.

It's worth noting that this practice does not require anything from you other than simply noticing the urge to procrastinate and learning what you can from the experience. You may find there are particular messages or false beliefs that contribute to your procrastination. That's good information to unpack later, but this exercise itself doesn't require that you ultimately resist the urge to procrastinate. That's up to you. Instead, the practice invites you to look more directly at the experience, simply noticing it with nonjudgmental awareness and seeing what you can learn from it.

1. To prepare for this practice, you may find it helpful to set reminders on your phone to recommit yourself to the practice throughout the day. The urge to procrastinate doesn't come on like a light switch. You may only notice it once it's bubbled up to the surface or, worse, when the procrastination has already begun. The idea now is to keep your awareness tuned into your urges to procrastinate throughout the day as they ebb and flow.

2. When you start feeling the urge to procrastinate, intentionally engage with it long enough so that you can feel it strongly enough to tune into it. When this happens, close your eyes and take a few grounding breaths that let you feel your connection to your body again. It may be helpful to gently rest your hands on your belly so you can feel your breaths as you focus your attention inward, trying to observe what you are experiencing in the present moment.

3. Try to resist the urge to judge. Simply notice what you can about what is happening in the moment. If you find you are engaging in a narrative, mentally note what the narrative is about. Resist the urge to engage in the narrative. Simply observe it long enough to learn what you can from it, challenging yourself to continue scanning the rest of your experience for additional information.

4. Eventually, you will make a choice about how to respond to the moment. You may choose to push forward with the task. You may choose to engage in a distraction. But the point is that now you are *choosing* to respond instead of reacting out of habit. That's a game-changing step in the right direction.

5. Learn what you can from the situation. Take note of it and move on. Unpack it later if you wish, but for now make a choice and move on.

STREAM-OF-CONSCIOUSNESS JOURNALING

If you tried the previous practice, you probably found that there is a lot to unpack in those moments when you procrastinate. Sometimes, as a result of these sessions, you may be left wanting to explore certain things in more depth—the pieces that feel sticky or mysterious to you. When this happens, it makes sense to carve out some time to intentionally deepen your exploration of these topics. One of the most useful ways to do this is through stream-of-consciousness journaling. Readers of Julia Cameron's seminal book on creativity, *The Artist's Way*, will recognize the roots of this practice as the morning pages exercise introduced in her book.

To prepare for this practice, get a pen and paper. Also get a timer and set it for however much time you want to devote to this exercise. You may wish to begin with 15 or 30 minutes. Choose whatever length of time feels right to you.

1. Once you start the timer, start moving your pen. Don't stop writing until the timer dings again. You can write about whatever you want; just keep writing.

2. When you notice that you've stopped moving your pen or you are otherwise lost in thought, don't worry about any of the writing that came before that moment. Simply pick up your stream of consciousness from exactly where you are and continue to document it one word at a time. Continue writing in this way for a few minutes before proceeding to the next step.

3. Now allow your mind to wander around the topic you wish to explore more deeply. Just start writing and don't worry about any of it making sense. Your spelling doesn't matter. Your handwriting doesn't matter. No one needs to be able to decipher any of it except for you. For now, simply document your stream of consciousness as best you can.

4. For the duration of the practice, continue writing. Keep bringing yourself back to the topic you wish to explore and documenting your thoughts about it. You don't need to make sense of any of it for now. All that comes later.

5. Once you are finished and the timer dings, fold up what you've written and set it aside. I recommend leaving it alone for at least 24 hours. You want to delay reviewing it so you can get some distance from and perspective on the content.

6. After you get some distance, open up your writing with a highlighter in hand. Highlight (or circle if you don't have a highlighter handy) the statements that stand out to you that seem to have some clarity or insight. You may wish to repeat this journaling practice with any of the themes that came up, continuing the conversation with yourself across time and learning from it.

KEY TAKEAWAYS

▶ Procrastination is an especially difficult habit to break. There are a lot of ways the deck can seem stacked against us.

▶ One key tool in overcoming procrastination involves regulating your emotions and tolerating any emotional distress that comes up when you approach the task at hand.

▶ Mindfulness meditation can be a valuable tool not only for emotion regulation and tolerating emotional distress, but also for all aspects of procrastination. Mindfulness meditation can have a powerful impact on setting you up for success in real and actionable ways.

CHAPTER 6

DELAYING GRATIFICATION

In this chapter, we'll discuss how mindful willpower can help us fight the pull of instant gratification in everyday life. We'll explore what instant gratification is and why we, as humans, are so vulnerable to it. You'll also learn several practices you can use to increase your chances of success at delaying gratification. These skills can help you bridge the gap between inspiration and action and more easily and effectively accomplish what you intend.

GIVING IN TO GRATIFICATION

Gratification is a word that describes the unique kind of pleasure you experience when a desire is fulfilled. When browsing lists of habits of successful people, the ability to delay gratification is generally toward the top of the list. It's easy to see how the ability to delay gratification and "keep your eye on the prize" is essential for anyone wanting to achieve much in life. The ability to control choices in any given moment and be clear about motivations and intentions is a trait that, if packaged in pill form, would be flying off the shelves.

Sigmund Freud believed people were guided by two basic principles: the *pleasure principle* and the *reality principle*. The pleasure principle is what motivates children. It is the drive to seek pleasure and pleasure alone without thinking about consequences. The reality principle is what we (ideally) eventually grow into as adults. It reflects our awareness of our place in the outside world and our ability to see beyond instant gratification. The idea is that as we mature, we become more and more motivated by the reality principle, leaving the pleasure principle behind. Now I can't mention Freud without also noting that a lot of his theories are outdated and somewhat questionable. But at the core, *some* of his ideas ring true, and this model makes sense on an intuitive level.

What's wrong with a little pleasure anyway? Isn't that what makes life worth living? Pleasure is certainly a fine thing to pursue, as long as it doesn't get in the way of greater long-term rewards. But as we just learned in chapter 6, instant gratification is a huge contributor to procrastination. Approaching a task that we feel the urge to procrastinate on can cause discomfort, to say the least. If we have the opportunity for instant gratification, it comes down to the choice between discomfort or pleasure. The choice of pleasure seems easy. But when we spend all our time avoiding discomfort or pain, all our choices become avoidance-based. This makes it really hard to remember what we were motivated by in the first place.

It's easy to fall into the trap of making decisions based on what you're trying to avoid rather than what you're aiming for. Running away from something and running toward something look quite similar but feel quite different.

A child's ability to trust promises made to them greatly impacts their future ability to experience the rewards that come from delayed gratification. As we all know, when humans are rewarded for a behavior, they tend to repeat it. This is especially true in children, who are primarily motivated by the pleasure principle. And when you practice something, you get better at it—especially when your brain is still forming.

Let's take a hypothetical example of two children from different households: Jeff and Joni. Both are saving their small weekly allowance to buy a toy that costs $50. Their parents have offered each of them a deal: If they save up $25, the parents will cover the other half. When Jeff tells his parents he's saved enough, they follow through on their promise and take him to the store to buy his toy. Jeff's delayed gratification was ultimately rewarded. But when Joni tells her parents that she saved enough, Joni's father takes the money and ends up spending it on something else. Joni was not rewarded, and she's much less likely to practice delaying gratification in the future.

It's also important to note the role that privilege (or lack thereof) plays in the complicated relationship between people and their ability to delay gratification. Children who are privileged enough to live in households where their basic needs are met often have more opportunities to practice delaying gratification. Let's take, for example, two hypothetical unrelated children named Maria and Asher. Maria has never had to worry about getting enough food at dinner. She also knows that if she is patient and displays good manners, resisting the urge to grab at food quickly, she is likely to receive a dessert at the end of the meal. Asher, on the other hand, comes from a family where there is rarely enough food to go around. He's hungry, and he knows that the faster he can grab at the food when it lands on the table, the greater the chances are that he will get something. Asher doesn't get a chance to practice delayed gratification. In fact, the only way for him to get a reward is to react as quickly as possible *without* delaying.

WAITING IS THE HARDEST PART

As simple as Freud's pleasure principle and reality principle are, they can give us the mistaken view that the ability to delay gratification simply increases as we get older. But as we all know, we don't automatically gain the ability to delay gratification as soon as we hit some magical age. No matter where we are in our lives, we always seem to encounter novel challenges that require us to delay gratification. When you're a kid, impulse-spending your allowance usually results in the need to delay buying a toy. But when you're an adult, misspending your money can have much more serious consequences.

Wouldn't it be nice if we simply gained the ability to delay gratification as we age? In some ways we do, as the prefrontal cortex, where impulse control lives, is the last part of the brain to finish growing. In fact, it doesn't fully finish growing until we are in our early 20s. This explains, in part, a lot of questionable choices teenagers tend to make. Neurologically, we don't finish building the tools we need to delay gratification until we are at least in our early 20s. But simply reaching your 20s doesn't mean you are now suddenly a master of delaying gratification. You still have to do the heavy lifting yourself.

And the need for heavy lifting abounds! Your day is packed with situations requiring you to resist the pull of instant gratification. These situations slowly drain your willpower reserves throughout the day. Much like how people looking to conserve electricity scour their houses for phantom power drains, it's important to identify the situations in your life that pull at your willpower reserves. As your willpower goes down, your ability to resist instant gratification is weakened.

To better understand the constellation of factors working against us, let's take a close look at one of the biggest phantom drains in most of our lives: our smartphones. Although the phone is just one example of willpower drain, it's a good one to unpack to bring into focus some of the factors working against us when it comes to avoiding instant gratification.

Our phones diminish our ability to delay gratification as we get hooked on their tempting siren call of instant gratification in the same way that we get hooked on slot machines. We get hooked on both things by way of an *intermittent reinforcement cycle*, which makes them especially difficult habits to break.

Reinforcement cycles are one way to describe how a behavior is taught (and untaught). If I wanted to teach an animal to push a button using a continuous reinforcement cycle, I would reward them with a treat every time they pressed the button. Behaviors taught this way are both learned quickly and unlearned quickly (if you stop offering the reward). But with an intermittent reinforcement cycle, the reward isn't consistent. Sometimes the button produces a treat, sometimes it doesn't. This kind of learning is usually associated with signs of distress and anxiety, especially once the reward stops coming. Once the reward is withdrawn, it takes a long time for the animal to stop frantically pushing the button and checking it.

Dopamine is a neurotransmitter that's associated with pleasure and reward. *It feels good* and is associated with addictive substances like cocaine. Every time you look at your phone and you see a notification, or a headline you like, you get a little dopamine hit. But more often than not, especially when you check your phone frequently, you don't see a notification. You start getting rewarded for checking your phone on an intermittent reinforcement cycle, sometimes getting that dopamine hit and sometimes not.

Because your smartphone's relationship with dopamine is so strong, it offers businesses countless opportunities to capitalize on your vulnerability to getting hooked. This makes your phone a heavy hitter in the collection of factors challenging your efforts to keep your eye on the prize and resist the lure of instant gratification.

Social media is especially problematic. Not only does it give us addictive dopamine hits through comments and notifications delivered on an annoyingly intermittent reinforcement cycle, but it also has a dark side of subtly (or not so subtly) blasting us with messages about who we are supposed to be and gives us a firehose of "shoulds" for our attention to contend with. All these comments, notifications, and messages play on our basic human need to belong and connect with people.

As a life coach and therapist in the busy city of Seattle, I've worked with social media influencers. For most, there's a stark contrast between the life they're living publicly online and what is really happening in their lives. As social media consumers, we scroll through images of people whose lives *seem* better than ours, and we're left with messages of where we're lacking and what we're doing wrong. It can lead us tumbling down rabbit holes of problem-solving or self-shaming, further exhausting us and distracting us from what we were trying to do in the first place.

The invention of smartphones has exponentially increased the opportunities for instant gratification. They offer myriad distractions with the promise of instant reward. Purchasing is as easy as clicking a button or two on your phone. And now, with virtual assistants like Amazon's Alexa and Apple's Siri, you don't even need to pick up your phone. You can just announce your intentions into the air, and the purchase is made and will arrive on your doorstep soon. Instant gratification is having its heyday—at your expense.

The following meditation is designed to help you learn how to tolerate the natural discomfort associated with delaying gratification. The better you get at delaying gratification, the easier it gets to avoid procrastination and accomplish what you set your mind to. It involves working to deepen your acceptance of what is. Naturally, this meditation includes the necessary component of self-compassion because, as the Buddha said, if your compassion does not include yourself, it is incomplete.

MINDFUL ACCEPTANCE

There are many versions of the old saying, "suffering equals pain times resistance." Or to quote writer Haruki Murakami, "Pain is inevitable. Suffering is optional." In other words, the more we *resist* the present moment, including pain, the more we *suffer*. One component of reducing resistance to the present moment involves cultivating an attitude of mindful acceptance of the present moment. It requires a radical and complete acceptance of what is. This includes a wholehearted *acceptance of yourself*, exactly as you are—someone who is a work in progress, just like everyone else.

I wish to take a moment, though, to clarify the distinction between acceptance and agreement. For example, I can accept the reality of the present moment, even though I may disagree with certain choices made by various people in leadership. I accept reality as it is even if I do not agree with or condone the behavior of those leaders. This also doesn't mean I won't be fighting for what I believe. It's essential for you to know that mindful acceptance does not stand in the way of mindful action. Here I am speaking simply to the practice of accepting of *what is*.

For more information about mindful activism, I invite you to look into the work of Zen teacher Thich Nhât Hanh. His foundation has multiple resources available. (See the Resources section on page 156.)

1. Close your eyes and take a few grounding breaths. Allow your attention to focus on your body's experience of the present moment with nonjudgmental awareness.

2. Notice when your mind wanders. Practice simply accepting whatever the distraction is with nonjudgmental awareness. This means accepting that your experience is your experience, and you don't have to do anything with it or about it.

3. As you practice, try to also notice how it feels in your body. See if you can notice any reactions or changes and observe your sensory experience of the present moment.

4. Continue to practice focusing your attention on the present moment and accepting whatever comes up on a moment-by-moment basis. Make sure there is a general attitude of acceptance, including of yourself. And continue tracking your body's experience of the whole process as it unfolds.

FLEXING YOUR IMPULSE CONTROL

Follow-up studies to the famous marshmallow experiment described in chapter 2 have shown us that the children who were able to delay gratification when they were young tended to grow up to be more successful in many areas of their life, ranging from financial success to overall satisfaction in life, compared to children who weren't able to delay gratification. Clearly, the ability to resist and delay instant gratification can be beneficial in many areas of our lives.

One shadow of the marshmallow experiment, however, is that many people have gotten the idea that the ability to delay gratification is a stable trait. In other words, you've either got it or you don't. But this isn't true. Just because people tend to stay on a certain trajectory throughout their life, it doesn't mean that the trajectory can't be changed. When you really look at the research, there is overwhelming evidence supporting the idea that delaying gratification is not just an inborn trait; it's something that is malleable over time.

Thanks to neuroplasticity, we know that we can literally change our brain and the way it functions based on what we pay attention to. What we practice is what our brain adapts to support. By practicing new habits around impulse control and delaying gratification, you can change your trajectory and build up your ability to delay gratification and enjoy all the benefits that seemed available to the children who waited to have their two marshmallows.

The problem is that, as we saw earlier in this chapter, delaying gratification can be really hard. It's important to arm ourselves with the tools necessary to overcome the temptations of instant gratification so we can honor our commitments to our future selves and follow through with our goals and intentions. One of these tools involves understanding what psychologists and other scientists have identified as some of the hidden forces at play impacting our ability to delay gratification in a given moment. Let's take the average trip to the grocery store, for example.

Grocery stores are intentionally designed to capitalize on our weaknesses when it comes to impulse control. There are so many temptations! Foods come in packages with labeling designed to highlight the very things that the manufacturers want us to think we need. For these products, there is a team of people whose job is to imagine what the typical shopper's vulnerabilities are and to capitalize on them. They want to convince you that you need it, to not think too much about it, and to purchase it immediately.

Another example lies in just one aspect of this marketing industry: the science behind pricing practices. The price you see on a label isn't simply determined by how much it cost the manufacturer to produce the item. A lot goes into the decision of how much an item should cost. The people making these decisions are well versed in the psychology of decision-making and impulse control, and they are ready to capitalize on it in whatever way they can. There are certain biases humans tend to have that are well-known in the marketing world.

No matter how much we understand how to apply impulse control, bringing that awareness to real-life choices is a different story. This is where the rubber hits the road, so to speak, on following through on whatever long-term goals you may have. If you can notice the moment when you feel the urge to procrastinate, you create an opportunity to more intentionally respond. Doing so bolsters your efforts to delay gratification and act in the interest of your longer-term goals. Let's try an exercise designed to bring mindful awareness to your grocery shopping or wherever you need to practice impulse control in your daily life.

YOU AND YOUR FUTURE SELF

Developing a relationship with your *future self* can have a huge impact on your ability to follow through with things. In one scientific study published in the *Journal of Marketing Research*, participants in a virtual reality setting were shown images of themselves that were technologically enhanced to make them look older. They experienced it like looking in a mirror reflecting the selves they would become. These participants interacted with their future selves through the virtual mirror. The participants who spoke to their future selves ended up saving a lot more for retirement than those who didn't interact with their reflected older self. This is a meditation designed to help you develop a relationship with your future self so you can enhance your chances for success at following through with whatever you set out to do in the future.

1. Begin by finding a quiet place where you're unlikely to be disturbed for a few minutes. Sitting is ideal, but there is no reason why you can't meditate while standing. Close your eyes and take a few grounding breaths. Try to notice how your body experiences the breath in the present moment. Feel the sensations associated with it and observe them one moment at a time.

2. Notice when your mind wanders to other things. Note the distraction with nonjudgmental awareness and gently focus your attention back on the present moment. Practice this step for a few minutes until the mental chatter quiets down enough so you can focus.

3. Bring into your mind's eye the mirror you look into most often. Try to imagine that it is directly in front of you as if you were experiencing it in a dream. See the room around the mirror and try to imagine it is really happening.

4. Take a look at your image in the mirror but try to imagine what you would look like several years older. Feel free to go as old as you want. Just pick a future age and imagine what your face would look like at that age. Be kind to yourself; this isn't about judgment. In fact, feel free to pick an image that you think would be the result of healthy choices between now and that future. Let yourself see a "you" that you would be proud of.

5. Now take a moment to imagine what you would like to promise to that future you. What steps would you need to take to get there? Allow yourself to imagine looking that future you in the eye and making a solemn oath to make your promises materialize and be your reality in the future. Take your time with this. It's not about imagining it quickly and moving on. It's about sitting with the feelings you observe in the moment when you imagine making these commitments to yourself. You are explicitly practicing intention setting.

THE MINDFUL WAY

Mindfulness can be a powerful ally in your efforts to delay grat-ification and manifest your larger goals. As we saw in chapter 4, nonjudgmental awareness and the ability to reflect on past mis-takes with self-compassion allow us to unlock the treasure chest of learning opportunities available to us in the present moment. Mindfulness meditation is essentially the practice of cultivating nonjudgmental awareness of the present moment as it is unfold-ing in front of us. That allows us to access the data in as unbiased a way as possible so that we can learn from our past mistakes (and successes). But that's not the only way mindfulness helps. It also helps us recognize our habitual automatic reactions to the outside world.

One automatic thought common in most humans is that pain and discomfort are to be avoided as much as possible. We are hardwired that way. But sometimes we can fall into habits of overemphasizing the need to avoid discomfort or pain and this can make us vulnerable to giving in to choices that pull us off the wagon, so to speak, of our good choices. In other words, we can self-sabotage. Sometimes we need to recalibrate our tolerance levels. Mindfulness meditation offers us the unique lens of get-ting curious about our discomfort as opposed to instantly falling into old habits of avoiding it at all costs. In many cases, some discomfort is the right choice. How revolutionary!

Let's take, for example, the ill-advised choice of going grocery shopping when hungry. Or perhaps grocery shopping took longer than you had intended, and now you're ravenous and waiting in line gazing longingly at the candy bars in the rack next to you. You know why those were placed there, don't you? Exactly for someone like you, who is vulnerable because you're hungry and tempted to make a choice that you know you'll regret later. You know you should wait until you get home, so you can eat the healthy food you just carefully selected for yourself. But this is not so easy with the potential of instant gratification staring you right in the face.

We've all had the experience of trying to save up our money for some long-term goal that requires managing our spending and applying impulse control strategically. Let's say you're saving up for a trip. You're trying to limit extra spending in an effort to save a few extra dollars so you can go on vacation. You walk into your kitchen with the intention of making a simple and inexpensive dinner, but then start thinking about how delicious Thai delivery might be instead. Soon, your fatigue and hunger take over and you find yourself, against your better judgment, picking up the phone and calling for an order of your favorite pad Thai and some panang curry. Unfortunately we often give in to old habits that work against our longer-term saving goals.

The following practice is another applied mindfulness practice to use *when the opportunity arises*, as opposed to when you've scheduled it. As soon as you find yourself tempted to buy an item that perhaps isn't the wisest choice, try applying the steps in the following exercise.

POWER OF PAUSE

This practice was written to be used in a store, but it could just as easily be applied to any situation where you're tempted to purchase something. It's all about injecting the power of pause into a potential impulse buy.

When you find your first item to purchase and pick it up, I invite you to pause, close your eyes, and take a breath. If you don't feel comfortable closing your eyes, you can shift to a soft gaze, looking toward the item you plan to purchase without focusing completely on it.

1. Try to recall, in your mind's eye, the thing you are hoping to save your money for. Give yourself a chance to recall it for a moment or two. Allow yourself to feel it in your heart, even for just a little bit. Remember why you want it. Don't worry about other people looking at you. They'll probably just think you're inspecting the item or reading the label.

2. Ask yourself what need this item in your hand fulfills. What are the motivating factors? What do you hope to gain from this purchase? Is it a necessity or a want? Why are you not choosing a different item? You don't have to dig too deeply here. Just pause and notice.

3. Try not to judge anything you notice. You're simply noticing and accepting, and nothing more. From that place of mindful awareness, you may choose to continue to purchase the item or delay it. If you choose to put it back, notice how you feel walking away from where the item was on the shelf. What are you feeling? Your only job is noticing here, and nothing more.

You don't have to apply all these steps to every item in the grocery store—you would never finish shopping if you did. It's more about looking under the hood of your spending habits. You'll get a peek inside to see what is going on, to access the present moment, so you can delay gratification if that serves your greater goals.

CONNECTING TO YOUR GOALS

Studies have shown that focusing on specifics around future rewards increases your chances of delaying gratification and ultimately achieving that goal. For example, if you really want to save up your money—whether it's for a down payment on your first house, a deposit on a dream trip, or college tuition—but you're standing in the store holding something in your hands that's tempting you to drain your bank account, close your eyes and imagine your future goal. This will help you put down the item you're holding. If you try to make your long-term goal more real in your mind, it will help you walk away from the item that is threatening your progress toward that goal.

The following meditation is designed to pave the way for clearer future decision-making. This exercise is meant to be practiced on a regular basis to help you build a relationship and association with your future goal. Then, it's up to you to practice closing your eyes and accessing it in the present moment when you need to. For the purposes of this exercise, we'll use the example of saving up to buy a bicycle, but you could just as easily adapt this mindfulness practice to whatever goal you want to accomplish.

1. First, close your eyes and let yourself imagine your future goal.

2. Imagine yourself enjoying your future goal. Imagine your new bicycle. Imagine the specifics about how it looks. What color is it? How many speeds does it have? Does it have handbrakes?

3. Now, allow yourself to imagine your day-to-day interactions with your goal. Think about what it might feel like coming home each day and being able to use your bike. Picture yourself riding it.

4. Let yourself imagine doing all the things you would enjoy most now that you have a new bike. Then take some deep grounding breaths and try to notice how your body is responding to the imagery. Simply take note, and nothing more.

5. As always, try to notice when you get distracted by other things and bring yourself back to the visualization of your goal.

6. When you are finished, try to visualize putting a bookmark into this imagery in your brain. The intention of the bookmark is so you can access this memory as viscerally as possible later, when you're tempted to set it aside in the face of immediate gratification.

KEY TAKEAWAYS

- The ability to delay gratification is not a stable trait. It can be developed over time.

- Delaying gratification is associated with a wide variety of benefits over the long term.

- There are many complicated factors at play when it comes to one's ability to delay gratification. It's important to extend the effort to make yourself aware of any blind spots you may have developed over time, including those that are the result of privilege (or lack thereof) you may have been blind to previously.

- Mindfulness meditation improves your chances of making wise choices in delaying instant gratification so you can accomplish your greater goals.

CHAPTER 7

REGULATING EMOTIONS

Have you ever felt that while your head wants one thing, your heart perhaps wants another? Sometimes our emotions seem determined to set us off course, waylaying our most well-intentioned plans. Fortunately, the relationship between our emotions and our goals doesn't have to be an adversarial one. Our emotional experience is an important channel of information, guiding how we should interact with the world around us. But when emotions run high, they can become overwhelming and blind us to the larger picture. Self-control can be elusive during those times. Your mindfulness meditation skills can be very useful in helping you navigate *emotional storms* with care and intention. This chapter will provide a background on what emotion regulation really is and why it can be so challenging sometimes. It will also provide several practical exercises to build your emotion regulation skills to strengthen willpower.

OVERWHELMING THOUGHTS AND FEELINGS

The relationship between our emotions and our actions is a complicated one that can cause humans quite a bit of distress. Strong emotions have an enormous impact on how we interpret the world around us and how we interact with it. In fact, it would be *difficult to overstate* the impact strong emotions have on us. Let's look at a typical real-life scenario.

Imagine for a moment that you are out for a walk and you notice a friend walking toward you on the opposite side of the street. You smile and wave. They appear to see you, but they don't acknowledge your wave in any way. So far this is neutral information, just the facts. But how you're feeling in that moment will have a big impact on how you interpret that situation.

What if you're having a hard day, for example? What if you're feeling blue or anxious or insecure? Most likely, you'll assume that you have done something to upset that person, or you will perhaps come to the conclusion that you misinterpreted their friendship and it wasn't really as strong as you thought. As you walk away, you assume these interpretations to be truth. This situation gets filed away in your long-term memory for future retrieval with the tag #EvidenceOfMyFailures.

But what if you were in a good mood? You might laugh and assume the sun got in their eyes or they were distracted, and you would enjoy having a laugh with them about it later. Your emotional state has a big impact on how you interpret the world around you. Why is that anyway? To understand where you start connecting emotions to your sensory experiences, you need to start in the room where it happens: your brain.

When you're experiencing strong emotions, your body releases certain hormones and neurotransmitters that affect your experience, along with your interpretations of everything.

If, for example, you're under stress, your fight-or-flight system may be activated. Once that is active, it has an enormous impact on the functioning in the rest of your brain. It basically takes charge, redirecting resources from the part of your brain responsible for logical thinking, abstract thought, and impulse control (the prefrontal cortex), and sends all those resources directly to your fight-or-flight center, which basically amplifies the primal and emotional response. This means that otherwise neutral stimuli will be automatically perceived as dangerous or threatening.

Have you ever gotten into a fight while on a date with your loved one? Have you ever noticed how quickly things can go from feeling friendly and safe to feeling urgent and like you are under attack? That's your fight-or-flight system kicking in and telling you that there's an emergency! You need to either fight back or escape the situation now! The stress response basically slips green-colored glasses over your eyes and gives you an Incredible Hulk–like response to everything. Once those stress hormones are flushed from your body, your prefrontal cortex can come back online and you can feel like yourself again and regain your self-control. The rebalancing is never as quick as we would like, though. Sometimes it can take a while for everything to come back to an even keel.

Given our vulnerabilities when experiencing strong emotions, it makes sense to arm yourself with the tools to manage them. Emotion regulation describes the ability to shift your automatic reactions to certain emotions and replace them with more intentional responses. In other words, it's about developing the ability to ride the wave of strong emotions without losing sight of your North Star. It's about the ability to remain cool, calm, and collected, even while still being informed by the strong emotions you're experiencing *at the same time*. You are aware of them, but you are also actively choosing your responses to them.

TRYING TO LET GO

Emotion regulation is difficult for many reasons, but it's definitely not impossible. We will explore practices later in this chapter that are specifically designed to make it easier for you to apply emotion regulation skills in meaningful ways in your life. First, let's look at some of the challenges we have when it comes to regulating our emotions in everyday life. Let's start with a story about sunglasses.

I used to have the best sunglasses. They had pink rose-colored lenses. I loved them because they not only shielded my eyes but also made everything seem beautiful. Even in the never-ending winters of my New Hampshire youth, the snow could become seas of beautiful pink waves. Until I took them off, of course, and my eyes (which had adjusted to the pink hue) now perceived all the snow as yellow, which was so very much less pleasing. The rose-colored glasses had their pros and cons, but I always appreciated the way they reminded me of how my perspective is always biased. It felt humbling in the best possible way.

Now, if you've ever worn glasses for a while, or even sunglasses, you know that it's easy to get used to the glasses you are wearing and forget that you are even wearing them. The same is true for the rose-, green-, or whatever-colored glasses your emotional state overlays on your entire experience. It's easy to forget about it and assume that what you are seeing is *universal truth*. In fact, you are always "wearing glasses" of some sort. You generally are blind to them, but they bias you and impact your experience. It's essential to try to remain curious and raise awareness about these biases, no matter how subtle. But it's also quite a challenge. It's hard to change something that you don't even see.

Another factor working against you, as I've already mentioned, is the overarching veto power of the fight-or-flight system in your brain. It doesn't matter what information might normally be coming from the rest of your brain, your fight-or-flight system is in charge when it's activated. Strong emotions trigger a sort of tunnel vision. When your prefrontal cortex (thinking brain) shuts down to only essential services because of the call to action sent out by the fight-or-flight system, it's hard to access the bigger picture, which is housed in that very same part of the brain that is shut down.

Let's look at another relatable example of how some of these factors can work against us. Let's imagine Layla, a single mom with multiple young children and an increasingly stressful job. At work, her boss has been increasingly rude to her, often yelling at her in front of coworkers. This treatment has left her feeling embarrassed and, at the same time, anxious. She finds herself in a mild state of fight-or-flight in between encounters with her boss, and is always waiting for him to swoop down and yell at her again.

Meanwhile, she's aware of increasing tension in her neck but hasn't yet connected it to the sense of anxiety (or the fact that her boss is a jerk and she should maybe consider getting a different job). She continues to operate under the cloud of this emotional state throughout her afternoon of picking up her kids, getting them settled at home, putting dinner on the table, etc. Throughout the evening, she experiences her children's requests as demands and reacts defensively. Her children react to her tone and experience emotional distress (read: yelling and crying). We don't need to imagine this scene much further before our hearts ache with compassion for Layla and her family as they all end up in tears in their separate corners throughout the night. If they had been taught emotion regulation skills and been able to practice them, some of this suffering could have been avoided.

One of the most powerful meditations I have come across for managing difficult emotions is the Mountain Meditation, which is a part of Jon Kabat-Zinn's mindfulness-based stress reduction (MBSR) program. (See the Resources section on page 156.) The basic idea of the Mountain Meditation practice is to apply an image of a mountain to your mindfulness meditation. You observe certain qualities of the mountain, like its strength and its stability, and try to notice these experiences in your own body. *Be the mountain,* so to speak. This, in and of itself, is a powerful practice. The following practice is one that I've built based on this original idea in an effort to help my coaching and therapy clients apply emotion regulation skills in difficult moments they often encounter in their lives.

PRACTICING EMBODIED RELAXATION

To prepare for this practice, I recommend you find a picture that evokes some memory of spaciousness and relaxation. It could be a snapshot of a beach vacation memory. It could also be an image of some artwork that evokes positive feelings for you. It could even be an image from a movie. You're looking for any image that you can associate with this feeling of relaxation, calm, and safety. Ideally, you would have a physical copy of it to support the practice as well.

1. Begin by sitting down with the picture in your hands. Let your eyes close and allow your attention to follow the breath. Try to simply observe how it feels to be in your body in this moment.

2. Notice when your attention drifts to thoughts, and gently redirect your attention to your experience of the present moment. Try to practice nonjudgmental awareness. Adopt a simple practice of noting your experience and then continuing to observe the present moment with nonjudgmental awareness.

3. Now open your eyes long enough to look at the image. Once you have a good visualization of it in your mind, allow your eyes to close again. Take a moment to bring your attention inward and notice the sensations in your body. How are you experiencing these feelings right here and right now? If the picture you're using comes from a personal memory, try to remember what it felt like in your body back when you encountered the moment in real life.

4. Sit in this way for several minutes. Follow a cycle of noticing your emotional responses to the image. When you find yourself distracted, come back to the image long enough to evoke the feelings in your body again and practice noticing and observing them as they change over time.

5. You may wish to visualize the feelings initially as a small ember that glows a bit brighter with each breath. You're trying to make room for the feeling to grow and take up more space.

When the practice is complete, it's time to take the practice off the cushion and into your everyday life. Use your image as a shortcut to accessing these feelings of calmness and safety when you need to regulate strong emotions. If you experience stressful Zoom meetings at work, for example, take your image and tape it to your computer monitor. When you start to feel strong emotions, look at the picture long enough to evoke the feelings in your body by association. Take a few deep breaths to make more room for the feeling. Slowly, your emotions will begin to regulate.

The practice of accessing feelings of relaxation and safety signals to your brain that the activity is an important experience and your brain needs to dedicate more resources to it. In other words, the activity engages neuroplasticity. Remember, *neurons that fire together wire together.* When you practice associating feelings with an image, connections between those things get hardwired in your brain. The image then can become a superpower, letting you access those valuable grounding emotions despite the overactive fight-or-flight system that may be at the helm of your consciousness.

AWARENESS AND ACCEPTANCE

One essential component of emotion regulation involves the ability to cultivate self-awareness, which is the ability to be aware of what you are feeling on a moment-to-moment basis without getting lost in habitual reactions to those emotional states. The foundation of emotion regulation comes from the ability to *simply name what you are feeling* in a given moment. There is an old saying in psychology: "To name it is to claim it." In other words, you can't own and wisely address an issue if you can't simply name it. Sadly, naming isn't a skill that is historically prioritized in the United States school system. I certainly don't recall getting much education about properly tending to my emotional needs when I was young.

Fortunately, we now have films like *Inside Out*, which I recommend to most of my clients as a starting point for understanding emotions. Dr. Paul Ekman, a psychologist and expert in emotions, consulted with Pixar to create this movie. (You can find a deeper exploration of emotions in Atlas of Emotions, a website co-created by Dr. Paul Ekman and the Dalai Lama, listed in the Resources section on page 156.)

Another standard tool I offer my clients is a *feelings wheel*. This is a tool I borrowed from the writing community but one that translates well to our work here. A simple Google search for "feelings wheel" will offer up multiple examples. At the center of the feelings wheel is a circle separated into pie-like wedges that list certain primary emotions. Each of these basic emotions is then broken down into more specific versions of the primary emotion. These emotion names are arranged in the second layer of a series of concentric circles, with each layer breaking down its base layer into more specific word choices.

To build your emotion regulation skills, I invite you to use this graphic representation, or another version if you prefer, to practice clarifying your various emotional states throughout your day. If you think you're feeling joy (happiness) try to specify which version of joy you're experiencing. Is it more enthusiastic? Perhaps proud? Let's say you identify your feeling as "confident." Now take it further. Is it more about being pleased or satisfied? The practice of pausing to truly experience your emotions and to

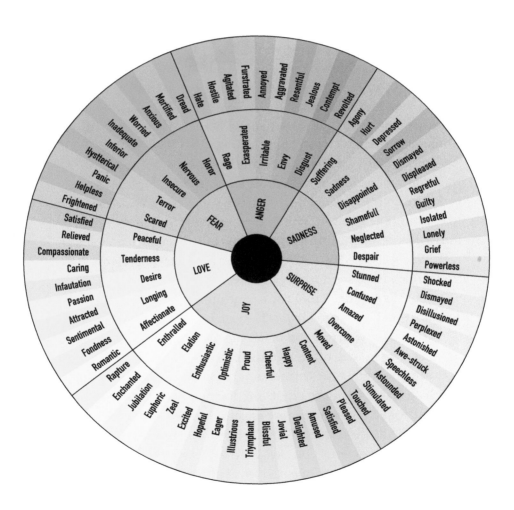

name them with nonjudgmental awareness can make an enormous difference in regulating your emotions.

It's important to note that you are never limited to one emotional experience at a time. In fact, experience proves that our emotional landscape is never black or white. It's also essential to practice self-compassion as you notice your responses to the experience of clarifying and naming your emotions. A lot can be learned from what you feel in the moment while naming your emotions. However, that moment is also a place where self-judgment can easily crop up. We tend to automatically attach certain judgments and stories to various emotional states. I'll offer a personal example.

Our everyday experience suddenly can become colored with a great deal of emotional distress. Many of us face challenges in our daily lives: the pressure of holding down two jobs, the difficulty of coping with a learning disability, the demands of taking care of a dependent family member, or the struggle of anxiety or depression. Despite the challenges we face, we're generally expected to carry on like they aren't happening, or like they're something that can easily be overcome.

When the day-to-day challenges of your life become compounded with unregulated emotions, it can be easy to interpret these problems as all your fault. This narrative often results in feelings of shame. When things seem to fall apart in your environment, it can feel as if your emotions go haywire, and you may perceive fires all around you.

The RAIN tool, or practice, has helped me through some difficult times. This tool has recently been made popular by authors like Sharon Salzberg and Tara Brach, but it has been shared by meditation teachers for as long as I can remember. The following is my interpretation of the practice.

RAIN

RAIN is another "off-the-cushion" or "in-the-moment" practice to apply when you're experiencing strong emotions. Once you are aware of the fact that you're experiencing strong emotions, find a quiet place and take a few grounding breaths. Close your eyes and focus on the present moment with nonjudgmental awareness.

Notice when you get distracted and bring yourself back to the present, again and again. Once you have done this for a minute or two, follow these steps.

1. Recognize what is going on. This means you simply try to name the problem for yourself. For example, "Linda was aggressive at work, so I'm feeling defensive and exhausted," or "My dad passed away this time of year and I'm feeling sad as a result." Try to just state the facts without judgment.

2. Allow the experience to be there, *as it is*, releasing the need to "do" anything about it. Simply call it out and practice noticing when you get lost in thoughts about *doing* and come back to letting the experience of the present moment just be *as it is*.

3. Investigate the experience with self-compassion and an attitude of kindness. See what you can learn, but be on the lookout for habits of "fixing" that may pull your attention away from the present moment.

4. Non-identification, or natural awareness, is the way you proceed. Natural awareness means observing what is happening without attaching stories to it or otherwise identifying with it. Allow whatever it is to just be as it is. In other words, adopt an attitude of curiosity.

5. Repeat the process as often as needed to ground yourself while you navigate strong emotional storms. You can think of this practice like an island that helps you catch your breath so you can continue to navigate as skillfully as possible.

THE MINDFUL WAY

As we've already seen, mindfulness meditation is associated with increased feelings of emotional stability and well-being. It helps calm our stress response system and allows greater access to the prefrontal cortex, which holds an essential role in regulating strong emotions. Mindfulness meditation and the ability to apply mindful awareness in the present moment can open the door to a world of useful information that helps us figure out how to better regulate our emotions.

Mindfulness, in and of itself, involves changing your relationship with the present moment. As you practice disengaging from habitual thought patterns that distract you from the present moment, you become able to see more clearly what's really going on without your vision being smudged or obscured by your personal narratives and judgment habits. This, in turn, paves the way for better emotion awareness and self-regulation. And *that* paves the way for increased willpower and better self-control.

We all come across what I like to call emotional storms. These are periods of time when our emotions run close to the surface, like groundwater. And when you add pressure and heat, emotions can erupt like geysers. We all go through periods of time in our lives like this. Whenever possible, it's good practice to treat these difficult times like the weather, with nonjudgmental, detached awareness. The weather isn't your fault. But it does impact things in real life. Sometimes emotional storms aren't your fault either. Sometimes they are a natural response to intolerable situations outside your control. Regardless of what created the emotional storms, mindfulness can help you weather them with resilience and strength, maintaining your willpower and self-control throughout.

One way that mindfulness helps is in its ability to clean your lens, so to speak. Earlier in the book I referred to *windshield wiper practices*. These are the practices you can apply on a regular basis to clean your lens, so that you can increase your chances of seeing things clearly and responding to whatever the present moment brings to you with as much skillfulness as you can muster to optimize your response. I recommend embedding windshield wiper practices into your daily routines so they become mental hygiene habits. For example, mindfully walk to the bathroom routinely when you're at work, or take a mindful breath before turning the key in your car.

The following is another "off-the-cushion" or "in-the-moment" practice you can use when you're feeling emotionally activated and need to regulate your emotions as quickly as possible. Like RAIN, this practice lists some steps you can go through when your emotional temperature starts to rise. It takes a slightly different approach, though. I often find that clients will apply both practices to different situations in their lives.

I invite you to try both practices and note how your experiences compare and contrast. Use what you learn to identify when to apply each practice in your life. The following practice is called STOP. It was created and popularized by Dr. Jon Kabat-Zinn and Elisha Goldstein, PhD, both thought leaders in the mindfulness world. The following is my interpretation of the practice, as I teach it to clients in my private practice.

STOP

This practice is meant to be applied when you're noticing some emotional distress. An example might be the moment of awareness in the middle of the night when you realize you have been stressing out about work needlessly. Another example might be when you find your interactions with family members so overwhelming that you shut yourself in the bathroom for a few minutes to get a chance to breathe. In these moments, find a safe space where you can focus on the present moment for a little while. Then follow the steps outlined here.

1. Stop whatever you are doing. Stop walking, stop talking, stop looking at your phone. Simply find a place to stop, and, if you can, close your eyes for a moment. A bathroom stall will do just fine, if necessary.

2. Take a grounding breath and reacquaint yourself with the present. Notice the feelings in your body as they come and go and evolve with each breath. Try to tap the brakes of your thought habits as best you can, coming back to the present moment with nonjudgmental awareness again and again.

3. Observe what's happening in the present moment with non-judgmental awareness. Try to name what you observe. Start with what you're experiencing internally. Perhaps your internal experience is one of anxiety or stress. Perhaps you feel under attack or underappreciated. Simply notice your internal experience. Then, observe what's happening outside of

you. Is it the middle of the night and are you in your peaceful bedroom? Are you on your commute unpacking your day? Observe any differences between your internal and external experiences. Try not to judge. Simply observe.

4. Proceed with this awareness. You can choose what you want to do with it, but try to maintain awareness of what is happening as you proceed with things. Perhaps, for example, you decide that when you are in bed, it's your time to let go of work and allow yourself some restorative rest.

GRATITUDE MEDITATION

There is a strong body of evidence telling us that a regular gratitude practice can help us feel less stressed and improve our general sense of well-being. Rather than mindlessly repeating the same things each day (like "I'm grateful to have a home and food"), this practice takes the power of gratitude and amplifies it with mindfulness. If you already have a gratitude practice, you can simply apply the following steps to your existing practice. If this practice is new to you, the basic idea is to identify a few things each day that you're grateful for and make note of them. Once you have something in mind, follow these steps.

1. State aloud, or in your head, something that you're grateful for. Be as specific as you can, and try to link it to something you directly experienced today, if possible. For example, it's good to be grateful for the fact that you aren't going hungry, but it would be helpful to get more specific. You might be grateful for a particularly enjoyable peach you ate earlier in the day or the way your first sip of water in the morning felt so quenching and refreshing.

2. Now, as you keep in your mind's eye the memory of the thing you are grateful for, try to bring some awareness to your body's response. Try to reaccess the feeling of gratitude you experienced in your body when you had the water or peach, for example.

3. Investigate the experience in your body with a sense of curiosity. You're not looking for anything in particular and there are no "shoulds" here. It's simply about taking the time to pay attention to something you are grateful for and, at the same time, observing how your body responds to that.

4. As your attention wanders to other things, try to gently refocus your attention on the gratitude. Give yourself a few minutes to honor whatever you are grateful for with your full and present attention.

KEY TAKEAWAYS

- Navigating emotional storms is tricky but manageable when you equip yourself with the proper tools.

- Regulating your emotions allows you to make more intentional choices about how you respond to strong emotions. With practice, you can change your habits built around how you react to situations and create more intentional responses.

- Mindfulness meditation helps us become more aware of our emotional responses. The practice also helps us disengage from unhelpful thought habits and judgments that are barriers to our success.

CHAPTER 8

WILLFUL EVERYDAY MINDFULNESS

By this point, you have a fairly full toolbox of ideas and inspiration to help you use mindfulness to develop your willpower and increase your self-control. Although it's one thing to understand these concepts on a cognitive level, it's a whole other thing to take that inspiration and convert it into *action*. This chapter is all about taking the concepts you've learned in this book and applying them to your real life so you can get on with making the changes that are most important to you!

AN EMPOWERED MINDFUL LIFE

We've learned that willpower and self-control are concepts that are more complicated than they might seem at first glance. When you really unpack them, it's easy to see that willpower and self-control involve a variety of separate but related skills. The ability to focus in spite of distraction, for example, is an inherent part of what we typically call willpower. We've also explored what goes into habit formation and how to intentionally change habits you've outgrown. We've looked at the complicated and somewhat symbiotic relationship between conquering procrastination and delaying gratification. We've also considered the power of emotions and the ways emotion regulation skills can help us stay on track despite the emotional storms that can sometimes throw us off.

By now you've also gained a good understanding of what mindfulness meditation is and how to practice it. You've learned a variety of ways to take a basic mindfulness meditation practice and apply mindful awareness to the situations in your everyday life where you feel stuck or stagnant. This is truly where your efforts to change can get some real traction. Remember that all change happens in the present moment. Our habits and thoughts tend to distract us and pull us away from the present moment. Mindfulness meditation improves our ability to access the present moment so we can make the choices and changes we intend to.

The power of neuroplasticity means that when you practice mindfulness meditation regularly, the parts of the brain associated with it grow stronger. Your all-important prefrontal cortex grows and becomes easier to access and use when you need it. At the same time, when you practice mindfulness meditation regularly, your brain reallocates resources away from the fight-or-flight part of the brain. This practice helps lower the volume of your emotional responses, making those emotional storms a bit easier to manage.

I've seen these practices work time and time again in real life with a wide variety of people in my private practice. So often, people come to me for help with making changes in their lives that they have been struggling to implement for years. When they're able to take the ideas we discuss and put them into action, I see my clients finally achieve success with making life changes. Change happens a little bit at a time, but eventually, as you gain mastery and trust in your ability to follow through with things, the ball starts rolling more quickly.

One of the greatest predictors of success that I've seen in my work with clients involves their willingness to make mindfulness meditation a *regular practice*. Of course, this looks different for every person. And that's fine. You have to find what works for you. Some people have more time than others. Some peoples' lives are more predictable than others. Some people meditate at the same time every day; others end up linking their practice to another event that regularly happens in their lives, like meditating after brushing their teeth in the morning. There is no perfect time or way to meditate. There is simply the way that works for you. And that way may change over time. I invite you to be flexible but consistent as you develop a practice routine that works for you.

You may find it helpful to get a dedicated notebook to track your journey. A notebook is a good place to jot down your ideas about when and where to meditate, and it can also serve as a useful place to capture your experiences with the different practices. Not every practice is going to be for everyone, but I invite you to experiment with all of them. Even if you don't choose to regularly adopt a particular practice in the future, there's something to be gained from each one. I encourage you to track your experiences in a notebook so you can reflect on them and build on what you know to develop a sustainable collection of practices that work well for you.

THE STRUGGLE
MAY BE REAL

One of the things that has continually amazed me throughout my many years of mindfulness meditation practice is just how easy it seems on the surface, and how this contrasts with the actual experience of it. Simply focusing on the present moment without adding too much judgment or thought sounds so easy. When you get down to it, though, it can be *really* challenging to practice. The power of monkey mind is fierce, and it can seem like your mind wants to do anything *but* focus on the present moment without judgment.

Then we have the weather—our *emotional weather,* I mean. Even the most skilled navigator can get thrown off course by a passing storm. The same is true with mindfulness. You might have the chops to tame your monkey mind in your formal practice, but when triggered by real-life situations, those skills you practiced on the cushion can feel distant and irrelevant. When you get triggered by strong emotions, your brain tends to reallocate resources away from the prefrontal cortex, where your deeper self-awareness and impulse control skills live. This is deeply problematic because we need those skills the most when we're passing through emotional storms. Fortunately, the very practice of mindfulness meditation has a positive impact on our ability to weather those emotional storms with resilience and strength.

Remember also that mindfulness practice is never about *achieving* anything. So as long as you are trying, you are doing it perfectly. The gains come from the practice itself, not from reaching some imagined landmark. Mindfulness meditation is more about practicing something that humbles all of us. It's about cultivating the ability to accept that experience without getting lost in our own judgments or narratives about it.

Think back to the mindfulness clock we talked about in chapter 1. In this model, 12 o'clock represents when you are truly mindful, even for just a moment. The rest of the clock walks you through the inevitable process of getting distracted, noticing you are distracted, and refocusing your attention on the present moment without judging it. It really doesn't matter how long you stay at 12 o'clock or how many times you go around the circle. It's about developing more awareness of where your mind is in a given moment so you can make more skillful choices about how to respond to that moment.

A common metaphor used in mindfulness meditation involves imagining that you're standing on a train platform, watching trains coming in and out of the station. Naturally, just because a train enters the station doesn't mean you need to jump on board. You would want to look at the sign on the front of the train indicating its destination first. But with thoughts, we tend to want to jump on board with whatever train is in front of us. That's monkey mind in action. Mindfulness is the practice of grounding ourselves to that train platform so we can be more conscious about which train we wish to board. It's also about developing the ability to get off a train we unintentionally boarded and have just discovered we are riding.

All too often, though, one train of thought tends to get through our filters and take hold. This is the narrative of self-judgment— look out for it. It tends to try to sneak its way into just about everyone's mindfulness meditation practice eventually. This is the voice that tries to tell you that you're doing it wrong, even though you've been making the time to practice. It might tell you you're not making enough progress or there's something inherently wrong with you that makes mindfulness meditation inaccessible to you. *Don't be fooled by this.* It's just another judgmental thought wearing a different mask or just another train to avoid boarding. It can be disregarded along with all the other thoughts you've been working with in your practice.

For many of us, the practice of self-compassion is easier said than done. For some reason, allowing ourselves the grace of being a work in progress—which is an inherent part of being a human being—can feel almost impossible for far too many people. Self-compassion is an integral part of mindfulness meditation, but it can be a particularly challenging aspect of it. Psychology studies show us that compassion practices are associated with a greater sense of well-being and emotional resilience. The following loving-kindness meditation is based on an ancient Buddhist practice of compassion meditation.

LOVING-KINDNESS MEDITATION

This practice involves cultivating a sense of compassion for various people in your life (including yourself). The meditation has multiple stages, and the order of the stages varies based on the teacher. Here is my interpretation of it.

1. To begin, find a comfortable position and close your eyes. Allow your attention to track the experience of your breath on a moment-by-moment basis. Notice when you get lost in thoughts and gently redirect your attention to the present moment without judgment, as best as you can.

2. Now bring into to your mind's eye the image of someone, real or imagined, you find it easy to feel compassion for. Try not to choose a family member, because feelings about family can get complicated. For the purposes of this exercise, choose someone you find it easy to cultivate a pure sense of compassion for. We will call them the "benefactor." Once you've identified your benefactor, offer them some well-wishes. Either say them aloud or in your head. You can choose phrases like "May you be happy, may you be well, may your life be filled with more peace." Choose phrases that feel natural to you and repeat them as needed.

3. While offering the well-wishes, also try to track the experience in your body. Try to notice what you experience in your body as you offer these well-wishes.

4. Now imagine someone you feel neutral about in a concentric circle behind your benefactor. This could be someone you don't know that well (like someone you share a bus stop with). Try to extend those well-wishes through the benefactor and beyond to this neutral person. Keep tracking the experience in your body in the present moment as it evolves.

5. Behind the neutral person, envision yourself. Offer yourself the same type of well-wishes and compassion you offered to the previous people. When you find yourself lost in thought or distracted, go back to the benefactor and cultivate the sense of compassion again, stretching it through the layers like a rubber band.

6. Behind the image of yourself, imagine someone you find difficult to feel compassion for. Don't pick the hardest person. You just want to think of someone you find mildly difficult to cultivate compassion for. Practice offering the same well-wishes to this person.

7. I now invite you to add the final layer of offering your well-wishes to the rest of the world.

By practicing compassion on a regular basis, and intentionally including yourself in the process, you are setting yourself up for success when it comes to buffering the fallout of emotional storms.

THE MINDFUL WAY

I don't believe that anyone ever has to accept something as simply a failure. Something is never truly a failure as long as you're able to learn something from it that you can use to set yourself up for future success. Getting lost in self-judgment or beating yourself up for mistakes serves no greater purpose other than to de-motivate you, which is exactly what you don't want to do when you have new information that can help you reach your goal.

Consider the tools in this book as the contents in your well-stocked toolbox, available for you to use whenever you need them. But remember, it takes a while for anyone to get proficient with any kind of tool. You've got to tinker and experiment with each of them to understand how you want to apply them in your life. In a physical toolbox, there are certain tools you want in the top compartment for easier access. These are your go-to tools.

The same is true for your mental tools. You'll inevitably find a few favorites and a few that just don't do it for you. I encourage you to tailor your toolbox in whatever way serves you best. Some tools may even be useful to write down on cards or take photographs of to keep on your phone, for example. You may also find it helpful to keep a list of the tools you have at your disposal, perhaps organized as formal (planned) and informal (in-the-moment) practices.

And remember that no one is expected to always be mindful—unless you happen to be on a mountaintop somewhere in a monastery with all your needs taken care of for you. In real life, most of us have to rely on creating *pockets of mindfulness practice* in our days to keep us grounded and clearheaded so we can make our long-term goals a reality and not get waylaid by the siren calls of instant gratification. It's all too easy to sail away on our own personal (and often negative) narratives and assume them to be truth. The further we go, the more we put blinders of bias on ourselves, limiting how we can experience and interact with the world.

I've saved two of my favorite mindfulness practices for last: mindful stretching and mindful housecleaning. These have been my go-to practices that I have most heavily relied on throughout my life as a mother, and especially during the months of sheltering in place as a family during COVID-19 in the city of Seattle. These are the practices I regularly employ to help me keep my lens clean throughout the days, staying as grounded as possible in the present moment so I can take wise action—one moment at a time—as the world changes in foundation-shifting kinds of ways. There's a lot you can't control in this world, but these practices will help you strengthen your ability to control your responses to what life throws at you. This is the essence of willpower.

MINDFUL STRETCHING

Most of us build up muscular tension throughout our day. Sometimes this tension can go unnoticed until we lie in bed at night and try to relax enough to go to sleep. I love to practice this meditation at night to let go of the day's pressures and tensions, both in my body and in my head.

First of all, only choose stretches that feel comfortable to you. This practice isn't primarily about increasing your flexibility, although if you practice it regularly that will inevitably happen. Above all, be gentle with yourself. This meditation is about releasing tension, not creating it. Don't do anything your doctor wouldn't be happy to know about. You may want to use a yoga mat or find an otherwise clear area your body can stretch in.

1. Close your eyes and take a few grounding breaths. Turn your attention inward with gentle curiosity, and investigate what it feels like to be breathing in the present moment. Try to notice when your thoughts distract you and gently refocus your attention on the breath *as it is happening right here and right now.*

2. Bring your attention to your body and how it feels in this moment. Identify a body part where you're feeling some tension.

3. Now move that part of your body to gently engage it in a stretch. As you lightly lean into your stretch, try to imagine the muscles in your body elongating as you stretch. Try to visualize the fibers stretching together in harmony.

4. Notice any tendency your body may have to pull back against, or resist, the stretch. I personally have noticed this often happens when I have gotten distracted by a thought. You may or may not have that experience. Either way, notice if your body wishes to resist the stretch and, if so, try to release the tension or ease back on the stretch a little bit.

5. Once you feel that those muscles were adequately stretched, scan your body and identify another part of the body that could use some mindful stretching. Think of it as a way to treat your body with loving-kindness before you turn in for the night. In the process, you are focusing and refocusing your attention on the present moment, paving the way for a more restful night's sleep.

MINDFUL HOUSECLEANING

I used to think there was no end to my housekeeping duties. And then I had children, and realized how naive my previous assumptions were about how much was too much housework. These already plentiful duties have increased exponentially as my family has sheltered in place together over the past several months. Suddenly, there are more dishes in the sink and more toys to put away. And no matter how hard my children try, they are young, and a certain amount of clutter is to be expected.

The last thing I want to do is cultivate negative or resentful thoughts as I pick up the extra detritus. Although it's true that in the grand scheme of things it isn't fair that I have more work to do around the house, in reality I need to accept that this is the case, and fairness has nothing to do with it. It's no one's fault. We serve ourselves well if we can use housekeeping to practice a little mindfulness instead of mindlessly building narratives that will cause suffering or destruction later on.

1. To begin, start anywhere in your home. Start exactly where you are, perhaps. Begin by closing your eyes and letting your attention follow your breath. Try to cultivate an attitude of nonjudgmental awareness of the present moment. Try to notice when you get lost in thought and gently refocus your attention on the present moment. Practice this step for at least a minute or two.

2. Open your eyes and look around the room. Try to notice any thoughts that come up and disengage your attention from them as you refocus your attention on observing the room around you with as much nonjudgmental awareness as you can muster.

3. Try to discern one item (that you have permission to move) that is out of place. Pick up that item and look at it. Identify what room it belongs in. If it belongs in the same room, skip step 4.

4. Mindfully move your body toward the room where the object belongs. Try to keep your attention focused on how your body feels as it is in motion. Notice when you get lost in thought and gently bring yourself back to the task at hand, simply moving your body to the room where the object belongs.

5. Once you arrive where the object belongs, look around the room. Again, notice any new thoughts that were sparked by entering the room and try to disengage from them with non-judgmental awareness as you bring your focus back to the room you are in. Try to identify where your object belongs. If you're not certain, place the object where your best guess is. Now identify one object in this room that does not belong where it's currently located.

6. Pick up that object and proceed to where it belongs and repeat the process. You are simply trying to be a body moving in space, slowly puttering around, chipping away at the mess one piece at a time. It is not about completing one whole room or anything like that. It's simply about puttering around and mindfully cultivating a positive home, one moment at a time.

KEY TAKEAWAYS

▸ Applying skills in real life can be tricky, but there are ways to set yourself up for success.

▸ Now that you have an abundance of tools, it makes sense to organize your toolbox to optimize its efficiency tailored to you and your own life.

▸ Self-compassion allows us to accept ourselves as a work in progress, which paves the way for learning like nothing else.

Resources

Books

The Artist's Way: A Spiritual Path to Higher Creativity, by Julia Cameron. The stream-of-consciousness journaling practice in chapter 5 of this book was inspired by the morning pages practice described by Julia Cameron in *The Artist's Way*.

The Bullet Journal Method: Track the Past, Order the Present, Design the Future, by Ryder Carroll. Bullet journaling is a customizable getting-things-done (GTD) system designed to help you focus on the tasks that are most important to you.

The Joy of Half a Cookie: Using Mindfulness to Lose Weight and End the Struggle with Food, by Jean Kristeller, PhD, and Alisa Bowman. This book outlines an evidence-based class designed to help people overcome addictive behavior patterns with food.

The Mindful Self-Compassion Workbook: A Proven Way to Accept Yourself, Build Inner Strength, and Thrive, by Kristin Neff, PhD, and Christopher Germer, PhD.

Websites

Paul Ekman's Atlas of Emotions (AtlasOfEmotions.org) website is a great way to broaden your understanding about emotions and how to develop skillful responses to them.

The Center for Mindful Self-Compassion (CenterForMSC .org) is a great resource to visit if you are interested in learning more about mindful self-compassion.

Dr. Judson Brewer's website (DrJud.com) is full of helpful resources around mindfulness and habit change. Included are videos of his popular TED Talks.

The Eisenhower Matrix is a popular time management and prioritization tool. For more information, visit Eisenhower.me/eisenhower-matrix/

Mindfulness-Based Stress Reduction (MBSR) is a popular evidence-backed program created by Dr. Jon Kabat-Zinn. It's a great class to take if you are interested in learning more about mindfulness meditation. For more information, visit MBSRTraining.com.

Mindfulness-Based Relapse Prevention (MBRP) is a class designed to help people use mindfulness to develop a healthier relationship with destructive or addictive habits. For more information or to sign up for a class, visit MindfulRP.com.

For more information about the Pomodoro Technique, visit Francesco Cirillo's webpage at FrancescoCirillo.com/pages/pomodoro-technique.

Thich Nhât Hanh is a Vietnamese Buddhist monk who is known in the West through his nonviolent social justice work with the Reverend Dr. Martin Luther King Jr. His foundation's website offers a wealth of resources for people wishing to deepen their meditation practice as well as engage in mindful social justice work. Visit ThichNhatHanhFoundation.org.

References

Alexander, Stephon. *The Jazz of Physics: The Secret Link between Music and the Structure of the Universe.* New York: Basic Books, 2016.

Baumeister, R. F., E. Bratslavsky, M. Muraven, and D. M. Tice. "Ego Depletion: Is the Active Self a Limited Resource?" *Journal of Personality and Social Psychology* 74, no. 5 (1998): 1252–1265. doi: 10.1037//0022-3514.74.5.1252.

Bowen, Sarah, Neha Chawla, and G. Alan Marlatt. *Mindfulness-Based Relapse Prevention for Addictive Behaviors: A Clinician's Guide.* New York: Guilford Press, 2010.

Brewer, Judson. *The Craving Mind: From Cigarettes to Smartphones to Love—Why We Get Hooked and How We Can Break Bad Habits.* New Haven, CT: Yale University Press, 2017.

Eberth, Juliane, and Peter Sedlmeier. "The Effects of Mindfulness Meditation: A Meta-Analysis." *Mindfulness* 3 (2012): 174–89. doi: 10.1007/s12671-012-0101-x.

Gailliot, Matthew T., and Roy F. Baumeister. "The Physiology of Willpower: Linking Blood Glucose to Self-Control." *Personality and Social Psychology Review* 11, no. 4 (November 1, 2007): 303–27. doi:10.1177/1088868307303030.

Goleman, Daniel. *Emotional Intelligence: Why It Can Matter More Than IQ.* New York: Bantam Books, 1998.

Hershfield, Hal E., Daniel G. Goldstein, William F. Sharpe, Jesse Fox, Leo Yeykelis, Laura L. Carstensen, and Jeremy N. Bailenson.

"Increasing Saving Behavior Through Age-Progressed Renderings of the Future Self." *Journal of Marketing Research* 48 (November 2011): S23–S37. doi: 10.1509/jmkr.48.SPL.S23.

Killingsworth, Matthew A., and Daniel T. Gilbert. "A Wandering Mind Is an Unhappy Mind." *Science* 330, no. 6006 (November 12, 2010): 932. doi: 10.1126/science.1192439.

McGonigal, Kelly. *The Willpower Instinct: How Self-Control Works, Why It Matters, and What You Can Do to Get More of It.* New York: Avery, 2013.

Mischel, Walter, Ebbe B. Ebbesen, and Antonette Raskoff Zeiss. "Cognitive and Attentional Mechanisms in Delay of Gratification." *Journal of Personality and Social Psychology* 21, no. 2 (1972): 204–18. doi:10.1037/h0032198.

Peters, Jan, and Christian Büchel. "The Neural Mechanisms of Inter-Temporal Decision-Making: Understanding Variability." *Trends in Cognitive Sciences* 15, no. 5 (May 1, 2011): 227–39. doi: 10.1016/j.tics.2011.03.002.

Rubin, Gretchen. "Are You a Marathoner, a Sprinter, a Procrastinator? Weigh In." GretchenRubin.com, Published June 3, 2013. GretchenRubin.com/2013/06/are-you-a-marathoner-a-sprinter-a-procrastinator-weigh-in.

Zahn, Daniela, Johanna Adams, Jeanette Krohn, Mario Wenzel, Caroline G. Mann, Lara K. Gomille, Vera Jacobi-Scherbening, and Thomas Kubiak. "Heart Rate Variability and Self-Control—A Meta-Analysis." *Biological Psychology* 115 (March 2016): 9–26. doi:10.1016/j.biopsycho.2015.12.007.

Index

Acknowledgments

My gratitude cannot be contained by the limited space I am allowed in this book, so I will need to be brief. To my husband, David, and my dear children, Henry and Meadow: Thank you so much for your support and fierce love. I couldn't have done it without you. To my family and friends: Thank you for supporting me from afar (I wrote this in the summer of 2020, when the world was sheltering in place due to the pandemic). Thank you to my clients for teaching me more about therapy and humanity than graduate school ever could. Thanks to Kurt, for introducing me to meditation. Thanks to Alexi, for reflecting my light back to me when I needed help seeing it the most. Thanks to Jessie, for helping me believe I could really be an author. And thanks to the amazing team at Callisto, for giving me the opportunity to amplify my voice and increase my potential positive impact on the world.

About the Author

 Samara V. Serotkin, PsyD, received her doctorate in clinical psychology from the California Institute of Integral Studies and her BA in psychology from the University of New Hampshire. Samara is a licensed psychologist and has been providing therapy and coaching to clients using a mindfulness-based approach for more than 20 years. Samara's work also focuses on the relationship between mindfulness, creativity, and self-actualization. She lives in Seattle, Washington, with her husband and two children. Find her online at SamaraSerotkin.com.